*Master
in the
Making*

Master in the Making

By Julie Ann Guthrie-Smulson

First Edition Print 2018

© Julie Ann Guthrie-Smulson

All rights reserved

No part of this publication may be reproduced, stored in a retrieval system, or transmitted in any form or by any means, electrical, mechanical, photocopying, recording or otherwise, without the prior written consent of the author and publisher. Reviewers may quote brief passages.

Names and identifying characteristics have been changed to protect the privacy of certain individuals.

ISBN: 978-1-7325520-3-6

Cover Design: Julie Ann Guthrie-Smulson

Editors: Julie Ann Guthrie-Smulson and Karen Tants

Dedicated to My Children

Acknowledgments

I would like to thank first and foremost a woman of many hats; my editor, book cover designer and publisher Karen Tants. Thank you for all the edits, messages and emails to complete ***Master in the Making.*** I am sincerely grateful to you for your hard work and healing.

I would like to thank the many healers who have helped me along my journey; you have all given me valuable lessons in also becoming a healer.

I would like to thank all my friends and family who encouraged me while I was writing. I must give a big shout out to Cyndee Woodward and John and Karen Nunes who provided support to me while I was writing. Thank you for being there for me when I needed to talk about my "spiritual awakening."

There were two people who gave me ongoing feedback and support while I was writing and editing: Phillip Berdion for saying that I was "Possibly the Most Interesting Woman in the World." I'm probably not, but it did encourage me to write. Dorenda Esparza you were the one who gave feedback on my writing, so that I could find my voice.

Lastly, I want to thank Oberon, King of the Fairies.

Contents

1. All Mixed Up   13
2. Undertow   26
3. Disturbed   41
4. Faith No More   52
5. Our House   72
6. Tell Me Something Good   76
7. Pieces   81
8. You Don't Know How It Feels   92
9. Photograph   96
10. Trust   118
11. Karma   124
12. This Is Your Energy   132
13. Good Vibrations   134
14. Back to School   138
15. Free Will   176
16. Suggested Reading   184
17. About the Author   185

Foreword

It takes great faith, courage, inner power, and inner strength to write from the heart the travails, trials and experiences of a life to share with others who may also have been through, or are still going through, similar challenging life circumstances. The road to self-mastery can sometimes begin on a twisting, winding path with occasional brambles, prickles and dead ends. It can take many years before that road begins to straighten out and become paved with the golden qualities of our inner true reality reflected outwards.

Julie's book shines a light on a taboo subject offering validation, self-care, self-love, and self-empowerment. In sharing her journey through life, Julie provides hope, strength, courage and a sacred space for others to heal. It is a soul-cleansing journey toward enlightenment and guides the reader to reach an understanding of the hidden power within that when accessed, can create transformative change within our outer reality, awakening intuitive perception, and leading to the realization of compassion, forgiveness and unconditional love. We can only manifest our inner warrior when we are standing in our own truth, looking out into the world, rather than in our own little 'ego bubble' with no care, compassion or consideration for others, or thoughts of helping anyone other than our own little self from our limited view of false reality. Julie's book *moves you*, way beyond the limitations of the *little self.*

Karen Tants-Healing Pen Publishing

Preface

Originally, the inspiration for writing this book was to share about the many supernatural occurrences I was experiencing. I have always been intrigued by the supernatural and I have wanted to write a book since I was eight years old. My supernatural experiences are one thing that spoke to me to write about. At one time I wanted to be a paranormal investigator before it became popular on television. When I discovered what dangers there were in paranormal investigating, I decided it wasn't for me. I have always been interested in the things we can't see.

As I was having these supernatural experiences and started my spiritual awakening journey, I realized the flashbacks I had of my Grandfather sexually abusing me were in fact my reality. I had done some research on child sexual abuse and found the statistics staggering. The statistics were only of reported cases. It was shocking. I felt that God had been calling me to write about childhood sexual abuse. Over the course of a few months it was revealed to me that many of the people around me had also been sexually abused. None of their cases had ever been reported. In each case, these people had been sexually abused by a family member. Sexual abuse is often perpetrated by family members or those known to the family.

My intention for the book changed again when I discovered that my ex-boyfriend was my soulmate. I wanted to dedicate the book to him. I felt God had used him to help me better my life. I was also feeling the call to help educate others about spiritual healing. I wanted people to know that the *reality* they were living may not be their *true reality*. I wanted people to know that they could be open to a *new reality*; or their *true reality*: The new reality where they deal with all the garbage in their lives, so that they can clear a path to live their full potential. I wanted people to know about the power of spiritual energy healing and how it could help them. I wanted people to know that they could end their suffering whether that be emotional, mental or physical. It's a different way to heal. It's not an easy path, because it requires a lot of change.

As I put pen to paper it was a difficult process to re-live all the emotions, feelings and thoughts of my past. I hadn't decided on where my book would end. It was possible that I still had some experiences to live out, to determine the end. Regardless of the reason I was writing this book, I knew *I had to do it*, and I had to publish it.

I attended the San Francisco Writers Conference. It was an interesting experience. On the one hand I was validated in the direction I was taking with my marketing plan. On the other hand, I learned I was committing 'no no's.' It didn't stop me. I learned that publishers don't like publishing books about abuse, and secondly, I had used Eat, Pray, Love as a comparison title. ("**Eat, Pray, Love**:" One Woman's Search for Everything Across Italy, India and Indonesia is a 2006 memoir by American author Elizabeth Gilbert.) You don't use Eat, Pray, Love unless you did exactly what was in the book. I was also having issues with just how crazy I sounded when trying to convey what my book was about. I had met a fiction writer, Dave Bartell at the Conference. We discussed our books. He said something to the effect, *"So you are going to try to change the way* *people believe? That's a hard thing to do."* It was a wake-up call, but I guess that was one point of my book.

I had put together a book cover and wrote the back of the book blurb and a short biography. I was proud of it and then I posted it to my social media. The simple act of doing that was, to me, an enormous step. I didn't realize what I was doing. I was exposing myself in a very personal way. The back of the book made me fearful of being seen 'as this completely crazy person.' I felt vulnerable, but I had to get over it. It was a small test for me to go the distance with what I had set out to do. I had to continue to write and disregard how crazy I thought I was coming across to the public.

Just prior to finishing my book, I started working with my editor, Karen Tants. Once I was done writing, I sat down to read my book. I really wasn't sure what the intention of my book was anymore. Not having an intention didn't stop me from moving forward. Karen was editing my book and I was planning to publish in the next two months. Karen pointed out some items that I might want to change, so I made some edits. All I wanted to do was just wanted to tell my story. It dawned on me that when I was three years old, the adults around me didn't want to hear my story and there are so many other stories like mine that never get told. It became that much more important for me to just tell my story.

Julie Ann Guthrie-Smulson

Disclaimer

The information in this book is not intended or implied to be a substitute for professional medical advice, diagnosis or treatment. NEVER DISREGARD PROFESSIONAL MEDICAL ADVICE OR DELAY SEEKING MEDICAL TREATMENT BECAUSE OF SOMETHING YOU HAVE READ IN THIS BOOK.

1

All Mixed Up

My story begins in my home office one lovely, sunny warm afternoon toward the end of February 2016. I was working as a Realtor in Modesto, California. A new agent with just a year in the business, I received a call from a new client by the name of Parker Timmermans. Parker told me he found me online; he had been in need of a mobile home due to his impending divorce and having to sell his home. Whilst on the phone with Parker, he suddenly remarked; *"Hey, you're 'kinda' hot!"* I was flattered, and I must admit I giggled like a schoolgirl as I let him know I was married. His words made me feel nervous, and even though it was only a phone conversation, I still blushed. He added; *"Of course you're married."*

Somehow, we ended up way off the topic of real estate. He told me that he played the drums; ever since I can remember I have wanted to learn to play the drums; my interest was piqued. I knew he was only telling me this to impress, but just the same, it made my heart beat that little bit faster.

He proceeded to tell me that when he was a teenager, he was best friends with Metallica's Kirk Hammett, and that he had also gone to school with Primus's Les Claypool. I am a music lover and had seen Primus in concert years ago. My head was spinning, and I was thinking, **"wow."** I hadn't met anybody in a long time who loved music as much as I did.

Later that evening, I received a selfie from Parker with a text, saying, *"to put a face with the voice."* I decided that Parker was a big flirt: *Obviously, you don't send selfies to your Realtor.* I looked at this selfie of Parker with his baseball cap on backwards and I wondered if he was bald underneath that hat: I thought to myself;" *"this guy has a big ego."* He looked like a short bald redneck. No matter what he looked like in that picture, he *absolutely* had my attention. I found myself looking at his picture often; I wanted to know more about him.

I tried to be professional and treat him as I would *any* new client, so over the next few weeks I texted him listings. I was a little nervous to meet this guy since I had never really dealt with a situation like this before. I was more concerned about my safety whilst showing him properties. It had taken me years to finally get my Real Estate license because of my fear of being hurt or injured. Deciding to be proactive about protecting my safety, I bought myself some defense spray. I also talked with a male coworker, Alfredo, about my situation. I asked if he would mind going along with me to meet this client and Alfredo happily added that our cover would be that I was training Alfredo to show properties. I investigated Parker's story and found that his house *was indeed* listed for sale. His story *did* check out, which put me more at ease.

I continued to communicate with Parker about available properties for the next couple of months. We had previously set up appointments to view properties, but for whatever reason, each time, he had cancelled these appointments. Parker didn't seem serious about finding a property, so I ceased sending listings to him.

'Fast-forward' to Mid-May 2016, Parker made contact again, wanting to see a listing in Oakdale. We arranged to meet at the home in Oakdale at 2PM. Parker called me around 1PM to tell me he was already there waiting. (My intuition told me that he was going to be there early.) Impatient, he told me to hurry up! There was a big part of me that was excited to meet Parker in person. I was nervous and excited, I drove as fast as I could.

Pulling up at the property I didn't see him at first, but I did see a black Toyota truck parked in front of the driveway of the mobile home. I can't recall the initial face-to-face, but I do remember I had trouble unlocking the door because my hands were shaking so much. My heart was beating fast and my mouth was dry. He walked nervously and very quickly from one room to another. I had on my professional persona, whilst looking for any potential problems with the property.

There was a weird, nervous chemistry between us. I was indicating different rooms where he could possibly put his drum set. *He was a bit shocked and surprised that I remembered he played the drums.* He wasn't thrilled about the mobile home; there was an issue with a section of the subfloor in the laundry room. I showed him another mobile home further down, but it was a new listing and there was no lockbox on it. He wanted to see the original one again, that we had come to see, and I was so nervous that I couldn't open the lockbox.

Eventually, we were finished looking at properties and were standing at the end of the driveway under the carport. *That's when time stood still for a moment and we looked into each other eyes.* He didn't look anything like the picture he sent me; he had these *large* brown eyes that could penetrate steel and a *full* head of soft, curly brown hair. He stood about five feet ten. His presence was soft and warm but also a little intimidating.

When saying goodbye, he went to hug me. We looked into each other's eyes. He saw I was hesitant about giving a full *body-to-body* hug, so he gave a half hug. I really didn't know *what* to think. This was the first time we had met, and I was his Real Estate Agent. *Who hugs their agent after the first-time meeting?*

A week or so elapsed before Parker's next call. He said that he needed to find a place right away because his house was closing escrow in thirty days. We set up an appointment for me to show him a property in Lathrop on the last Saturday in May. When I pulled up, he was sitting in his Toyota pickup truck that was parked right in front of the mobile home. My intuition told me he was drinking a beer out of a brown paper bag; and sure enough, he *was*.

He told me he had just gotten off from work and when he got out of his truck, he was still wearing his work boots, untied, with long socks that were pushed down above the top of his boot. I was checking him out as I followed him through this small, dark and small musky smelling two-bedroom. He had some *sexy legs*. I have always had *this thing* for calves, ankles and shorts with boots. I saw he was checking me out too. He looked me up and down and was licking his lips like he was about to devour a delicious meal. It made me very nervous. My insides were fluttering. I was in *giddy schoolgirl* mode again.

Master in the Making

The mobile home wasn't what he wanted. I locked the door and put the keys back into the lockbox. He seemed frustrated and I could tell he was getting very impatient with me. I told him I had printed out other listings I planned to show him the following day and asked if he wanted to have a look at them, to save him some time. He followed me over to my truck, I opened the back-cab door, pulled out the listings, and shaking again, handed them to him. I was nervous that he may abandon his search with me. He looked them over and seemed a little more at ease about viewing properties with me the next day.

I can't remember how we left each other that day, but I do remember feeling an electric, crazy, nervous energy about seeing him again. I was thinking about his curly brown hair, his big brown eyes, and *those* boots. I was so distracted and nervous as I drove away that I missed the freeway entrance, *twice,* and ended up taking some country roads back home. I was dazed and confused.

Later that evening, Parker texted me to confirm that we *were* going to meet. I don't know what I was thinking, but I sent him some Facebook meme about 'there's no whining' in Real Estate, but 'there's wine-ing' with a picture of a glass of wine. When I sent it, I knew I was flirting with him. He called me very quickly after my text. He asked if I wanted to go for drinks after we found him a place. I agreed to have a drink after we signed a purchase offer. We decided to meet the next morning at the Mall parking lot. He texted me and told me not to wear open-toed shoes. I figured out that he had a foot fetish and that's why he was practically drooling on me at the mobile home the day before; I had been wearing open-toed high heels.

Master in the Making

Parker called me and asked me about my 'back page ad.' I said, "what are you talking about, back page ad?" I had barely hung up the phone with him and I was thinking; *what ad? where?* His voice had cracked, and I knew he had figured out that he had called the wrong phone number. He had called me, and not a 'back page ad' phone number. I knew he was responding to some personal ad and he had called me by accident. I knew deep down inside that Parker was a lying, cheating player. His accidental call was just a confirmation of that.

That night as I lay in bed I couldn't stop thinking about Parker and how what I had done was very unprofessional. I could lose my license and my career if things went bad. This guy could blackmail me or worse. *I really didn't give much thought to my husband or marriage.* Weird thing is that I think I was more concerned about my job. I was enjoying the attention I was receiving. It was like I was getting a high from it. I hadn't done anything wrong at all, but I was starting to feel guilty.

By Sunday morning I was really regretting flirting with him the night before. We met at the Mall parking lot as arranged, and when he got into my truck, I asked him to delete all our messages. I didn't think it was professional of me, nor the right thing to do. I was married, and a Realtor. I had been married to my husband for twenty-one years and had two boys. My oldest boy, Alex, had moved out a year prior, and was turning twenty-one in two days. My youngest, Aiden, was to graduate high school within days. I wasn't completely happy in my marriage, but it was no excuse for flirting or even thinking about being unfaithful.

Master in the Making

Regardless of my feelings, I had a job to do. Parker and I ended up back out in Oakdale at the same mobile home park that we had first met in person. We had some time to kill before our showing appointment. I ended up driving around this area in the country and pulled over, so we could have a cigarette. I can't remember what our conversation was about whilst driving. We stood at the back of my truck smoking. He told me more about himself.

He said he spoke Farsi and at one time when the FBI and CIA were looking for translators, he had contacted them. He said he thought it would be a way out of driving a truck for a living. The only problem with that was that he did not know the Farsi alphabet, so they couldn't use him. He had to continue to drive a truck.

He was a hunter, a taxidermist, and an artist. He told me had been born in Belgium and that his mother was Iranian, and his father was Belgian. His father had been a scientific glass blower who had been contracted all over the world by various governments, corporations and businesses; one of which was NASA. His mother and father had met when his father was working in Iran.

His father had passed away from complications due to a glass blowing accident that damaged his lungs and later his mother tragically passed away from a diabetic coma. He had a younger sister. He had five children of his own; the eldest was thirty-four and the youngest, seven. He had been married twice and had two boys from his first marriage, and two boys and a girl from his second marriage. His eldest son was a movie director in New York and his second eldest son was in a band in the Bay Area. He himself had been in a band and had recorded a CD. His band had even had an article written in the San Jose Mercury Newspaper following the release of their CD. We talked about music, politics and our families, and discovered we shared a lot of the same views.

I showed him five properties, and when we were at the last one, he was enchanted by the ambiance the seller had created with lit candles and soft music playing. We walked around inside, and as I was standing there in this semi-hallway near the kitchen, the thought crossed my mind and my gut feeling was telling me that Parker and I were going to be a couple. It was my intuition. My rational brain was saying; "You're married and what is that all about, me and this guy are going to be a couple, what the hell?"

Parker being the impatient guy he is, was done looking at the home. He had previously told me that he wanted this one, but he wanted to leave so I remotely unlocked the doors and turned on the engine so that he had the air-conditioning on. I stayed behind because I wasn't finished asking the seller questions. I wanted to know when the roof had been done and if she had a copy of the mobile home park rental application. When I got back to the truck, he asked why I took so long; I wasn't even behind him five minutes. I explained to him that I had questions that were on his behalf. I wanted to make sure that the seller was going to send a copy of the mobile home park rental application to her Realtor and have her send one to me for him to fill out. If he really wanted the mobile home, we were going to need it to see if qualified to rent the space from the park.

We headed back in the direction of the Mall and ended up going to B.J.'s Brewhouse. We both ordered a beer, then I wrote up the purchase offer and signed it. He wanted something to snack on, so he ordered chips and Queso and some other appetizer. I can't remember much of our conversation, but I do remember him saying; *"You can't look me in the eye, can you?"* I glanced at him then quickly looked away. Taking up the challenge, I stared deep into his eyes until he squirmed and laughed. He asked me, *"What's going on at home with your husband? Why are you here having a beer with me?"* My heart kind of sunk. Was it obvious that I wasn't happy with my husband and homelife? I wouldn't have put myself in such a position with Parker if I *were* happily married. I excused myself and went to the washroom. I had to catch my breath from what he had just asked me and check my thoughts. At that moment, I did not care what I did or said.

When I married my husband, I was pregnant with my first son, Alex. I felt I was short-changed with not having had a lot of time to date my husband before we got married. Over the years I had this notion that once the boys were grown, my husband and I would start dating each other again. Well, it turned out to be just a notion that never manifested. In fact, my husband found other things to fill his time and attention and those things were not *me*. I was *never* a priority in my husband's life. We became like two roommates 'sharing space'. I shouldn't have had to wait until our boys were grown. We should have been dating all that time.

When I got back to the table I sat down and had a sip of my beer. Parker touched my hand with one of his fingers and he said, *"I touched you!"* Like a little kid flirting. I was taken aback. We sat there drinking our beer and eating the chips and Queso. We had silences, but they were comfortable and relaxed.

Master in the Making

Parker was very disappointed with the appetizer and began to talk with his best French accent as though he was a food critic: *"Dis, dis is garbage! Did you dig dis ships out of de buttom of a Tostitos bag?"* He complained to the waiter in the same accent and portrayed himself to be a food critic for the San Francisco Chronicle. I want to say they waived the cost of the chips and Queso. Really what do you expect out of Queso and chips?

Feeling a little bit of a buzz, I took him into my office. I had received the mobile home park application. I had to have him fill it out because he wanted and needed a home asap, and 'time is of the essence' in Real Estate. He looked like a bad boy. Well, he *was* a bad boy. I couldn't stop looking at him, the way he wore his tank top with his tan, muscular tattooed biceps, shorts and flip flops. He was just so cute and flirty. We sat in a conference room and flirted back and forth while he filled out the park rental application. I had to make copies for him but being an impatient man, he took off out the office doors to my truck before I was done. I chased after him.

Parker wanted to get another beer; for some reason we were buying beer from a gas station. It was Memorial Day weekend and it was hot outside. I was wearing black polyester slacks and closed toed black leather shoes. I don't know why, but I had brought some shorts and flip flops. I changed in the truck while he was buying the beer. There I was, at 46 years old, looking for a place to drink beer in an orchard in broad daylight.

We found a secluded spot in a walnut orchard. We talked about politics, religion, music and whatever came to mind. Then, all sudden I felt him behind me as he ever so gently took his left hand, turned my head so that he could have access to my neck and kissed me. He had his right hand on my right hand and touched it so very gently and sensually. He had this wonderful clean smell. I knew this smell very well, but I couldn't figure out what it was. It wasn't his laundry detergent and I wasn't sure if it was his aftershave, but the aroma was heavenly.

I got caught up in the moment. No other man had *ever* touched me this way. No man other than my husband had touched me in years. I let it happen. I was slightly buzzed and was enjoying myself. In my head, the 'little punk rocker with big attitude' was fighting the faithful housewife, and the professional Realtor.

Parker took it a little further and had his left hand in my underwear and his right hand pulling his cock out of his pants. I was a bit shocked at what had just transpired. I told him to put 'that thing' away and he did. Not five minutes later he was *again* pulling his shenanigans. This time I think I allowed it to go on a little longer. *"Parker! Parker! Parker! Parker!!! I'm not going to fuck you!"* I wanted to kiss him. I even wanted to have sex with him. My logical rational mind was screaming *"You're married!"* I couldn't allow him to go any further.

It was getting late in the afternoon and I don't know how long we were in that orchard. It must have been at least an hour or more. When we left, we headed back to his truck in the Mall parking lot. His hands were all over my right hand while I was driving. When he touched my hand, it was the most sensual, sexy feeling I had ever experienced. Nobody had ever touched me that way, ever.

Master in the Making

Somehow, the time we spent together that day had formed a bond between us. It was hard to say goodbye to him. We were mesmerized by each other and could not stop gazing into each other's eyes. It was as if we were both magnetized by an invisible force. I told him I didn't want to leave him, and he said he felt the same way. I had never felt that way about anybody else in my entire life.

I can't remember exactly how quickly we were texting and calling each other. I know that I had been working on his mobile home offer and had taken his mobile home park application to the park in person. His offer was accepted and his application for the park had been approved.

Beyond the matter of business, I remember a specific phone call that Parker asked me if I felt the connection, he had felt that Sunday and I had agreed that there *was* a connection between us. From there we texted and talked with one another and it wasn't about his real estate purchase.

I needed Parker to sign some documents about a week after his offer was accepted, so we met at a pizza place in Manteca. He had to have a drink as soon as we arrived, getting a small pitcher of beer. As he poured his beer, his hands were shaking. I thought maybe he is a little nervous around me. I also might have been lying to myself not wanting to believe what I knew about that shaking. I had been around many alcoholics in my family and the shaking was a telltale sign of an alcoholic needing a drink. I had suspected prior to this that he was an alcoholic; the shaking had confirmed it. My heart sank a little then, but it didn't stop me from being interested in him.

We talked on the phone and texted each other a lot during the next couple of weeks. One night around that time

Master in the Making

I met him at a bar in Lathrop to have him sign a document. Later that same night, he took me out to dinner. We were outside in the parking lot smoking cigarettes, when unexpectedly he put his arm around my shoulder and told me to look at our reflection in the truck window. He said; *"we make a good-looking couple, don't you think?"* From that moment forward, we met as often as we could. I lost count of how many times I had driven to Stockton to see him, but it was a *lot,* and within a short period of time.

I had a dream around this time; it was one of those dreams that had a message for me. I would call it a premonition dream. The gist of the dream was that I was going to be dead within six months to a year. I'd had these types of premonition dreams before, but this one was very heavy and carried a sense of urgency with it. Although the message was death, I did not take it that I was going to die. My physical death was possible, but I took it as though life as I had known it was going to completely change. I began to question my life. If I was going to physically die, was I happy where I was and with what I was doing? *"Was I going to die knowing that I had done everything I wanted to do?"*

This whole 'episode' with Parker was possibly just a whirlwind romance that would blow away tomorrow, or it would have been exactly what I had wanted in my life? Could *he* be the one? What if he *was* 'The One?' Would I be able to live with that? Parker and I *did have* that conversation about the possibilities of being 'The One.' Could I live with knowing that 'The One That Got Away'? Parker and I spoke of the possibilities of each of us being *the one* for each other.

2
Undertow

I had been thinking a lot about what Parker asked me that day at B.J.'s Brewhouse: *"What's going on at home with your husband?"* Was I truly happy? Was I just content? What was my home life really like? Things weren't improving between me and my husband. One night a few years ago I had packed up the kids and gone to stay with my parents; that led us into marriage counseling over what I am about to tell you.

My husband and his entire family were pressuring me to take care of my husband's sister, Marty, because she was sick with Multiple Myeloma. Nobody else in the family wanted to take responsibility for caring for her. Marty didn't want her teenage kids taking care of her. I refused to care for his sister. One of my other sisters-in-laws came over to tell me that I needed to do it and she went as far as telling me that I was "crazy" for not doing it for my husband.

My husband's family and I did not have a great relationship. His mother basically hated me from the beginning. I never gave her or anybody else in his family a reason not to like me. My husband would never admit to me that his mother never liked me. I always seemed to be the one who was blamed for any disturbance within his family. My husband never protected or defended me. His ties to his family were stronger than our marriage bond, and that hurt me a lot over the years.

Our trip to the marriage counselor concluded with me not taking care of his sister. In the end, if My husband and his family weren't going to help take care of Marty then there wasn't anybody who could insist that I do the job. I was able to tell myself that these people had a really different way of looking at things. I knew where my heart was in my words and actions, and it didn't matter to me anymore what his family might fabricate about me and blame me for. It still hurt me that my husband never found it within himself to defend me. As I matured in our marriage, I understood why he couldn't defend me; he couldn't even stand up and defend *himself.*

I thought about my boys and how they were both going to be living their own lives. They didn't need their mother as much anymore. I was looking toward a future that would be very lonely, with no children at home for much longer. My husband was so busy with his full-time job, his part-time eBay business, working on his car, and watching baseball. There were many times I would ask him to spend intimate time with me and he wouldn't because he valued his eBay and/or baseball games more than me. I wasn't a priority to my husband, at all. I was important to him when he needed me to buy the correct toilet paper or maybe to have somebody to glare at in the morning because there wasn't fresh coffee when he woke up. I had dealt with my husband's silent treatment and glaring at me whenever he was disappointed or upset or he didn't get his own way. It was emotional and mental abuse. His behavior toward me made my body tense up and sick to my stomach.

Master in the Making

My husband and I had unintentionally become roommates over the past few years. My husband didn't pay attention to me or show affections towards me. Over the past ten years I had tried to communicate with my husband how I felt and what I wanted. He did listen and tried, but that never lasted very long. The cold fact was that my husband was never going to change into the man I wanted and needed him to be. After thinking long and hard about all the dynamics and consequences of leaving my husband, I made the decision to leave. I had given him more than twenty-one years of my life to do right by me.

I knew that I would meet opposition from him and his family, and from my boys. I also knew that more marriage counseling would be brought up. I didn't want to deal with all the drama, the guilt trips, the endless conversations, and wasting money talking to a third party that would lead me right back to where I began; being unhappy and wanting to leave. I knew if my husband and I went into marriage counseling it would be fruitless; he would change momentarily, then everything would return to how it was. I was within three years of turning fifty. I felt like the time in my life was running out. I didn't want to waste any more time. I can't say that I wasn't scared of the financial repercussions, or that I wasn't scared to begin all over again. I *was* scared, but there was a part of me that was happy and looking toward adventure, and to my future.

It was a shock to my husband when I told him I wanted a divorce. I told him I wanted to keep it civil between us, and that I did not want his family involved. I did not want phone calls or visits from his family whatsoever like they had done with previous divorces in his family. He wanted to know if there was somebody else. I ended up lying to him; probably the biggest lie I had ever told anybody. I felt bad to a degree for lying to him. I believe I was trying to protect myself from any further abuse, because I just wanted out without a fight. I think in my mind I justified lying for all the bullshit I had taken over the years.

I wasn't going to bring Parker into our divorce, although he *was* the catalyst for me leaving. My divorce from my husband was about my relationship with my husband. I had given my husband twenty-one years and I was unequivocally done. Of course, marriage counseling came up and I refused to go. I suggested that he go to marriage counseling by himself.

My husband kept at me for a couple of weeks trying to get me to change my mind. To me it felt like a dog and pony show with a lack of sincerity. I was not budging one bit from my position on leaving. I was very confident and had such a conviction in my stance on leaving that I even surprised myself. My husband did go to marriage counseling and the counselor told him that I was done. To me the message he got from the counselor was a relief to me; a third party telling him that I was done and that he needed to move on. I encouraged him to do some online dating.

Within a month of being in that walnut orchard, I had filed for divorce, moved into an apartment and bought a new car. I wasn't as financially scared as I had been. I realized what my portion of the assets were. They were much larger than I thought that they would be.

During that month, Parker was having a hard time transitioning and I felt sorry for him. He had to move out and was going through some depression from the loss of having his young daughter and youngest son at home with him. He was also going through the loss of losing his home (in the divorce) that he had worked so hard to acquire. I was there as a Realtor and a friend to help guide him to get the everything finalized.

There was a gap of several days, when Parker's current home was closing, and his mobile home was going to close escrow. He called me and was very distraught. His voice was cracking like he was on the verge of crying. He was having a meltdown. His water had been turned off; he had been fighting the necessity to completely move out and he still needed to move his stuff to a temporary storage unit. At this point I told him he needed to get out, because he couldn't stay there with no water. He moved to a Motel in Manteca, close to his workplace. He wanted me to come to see him the first night he was there. I couldn't go that night, but I did go the following night and he took me out for dinner. I remember us kissing and hugging each other after we had dinner. I was finding all the running around very exciting and freeing.

Parker had moved his belongings into storage, but he still had a couple days before he could move into his mobile home. He had relocated to another hotel in Turlock where I went to see him a couple of times before he moved into his new home. Parker and I saw each other as much as possible. He was now settling into his new life, as I was also settling into mine. I felt a freedom, as if I was again living like I was in my twenties. My apartment had a wall air conditioner in the living room. It was summer, and I was on the second floor. I didn't buy a lot of furniture because I knew I was going to be moving and didn't want to have to move furniture up and down stairs. I did invest in a decent bed. I ended up moving my top mattress to the living room because the heat was unbearable with my hot flashes. It was so hot that I bought three fans and cranked that air. I didn't need a bunch of "stuff" to make me happy. I was happy with a mattress, air conditioning and being free from my former life. I was feeling independent. I was planning on doing the things I had always wanted to do. I was also wanting to do things that I had never done before. I was trying to figure out what I wanted out of life and who I was again. I was trying to figure out who I wanted to become.

I remember one dry, hot day in July; Parker and I went to the Dust Bowl in downtown Turlock to have dinner and drinks, we were really enjoying being together. My youngest son, Aiden, called me; he was on a road trip to Texas with some of his buddies. It was so good to hear from him. A part of me missed being in the old mom role, but here he was, two states away, having the time of his life.

I told him I was out having a burger with a friend of mine, which I was. While I was talking with Aiden, Parker was seated on a dried-up water fountain holding my hand and trying to pull me closer to him. I was trying to concentrate on my conversation with Aiden. It was daylight out still and families were passing by. Parker was looking at my body, as he put his legs out, wrapped them around me and drew me toward him; I allowed him to.

There were many more nights at the Dust Bowl in downtown Turlock with Parker. We would smoke cigarettes before and after our dinner; and we would wind up kissing somewhere in front a closed storefront. It was the most romantic time of my life.

Master in the Making

Another time we sat on his porch, which we would do quite often before we went out to dinner. It was late one afternoon and hot outside, but there was a cool breeze. We sat very close together and put out foreheads together and looked into each other's eyes. I touched his face very gently like a mother would to do to soothe a child. It was very intimate, and I felt very bonded to him at that time.

I had finally figured out that the scent he wore was called 'Grey Flannel.' It was one of my favorites. I had fallen in love with the scent when I worked for Bass Shoes in South Lake Tahoe. I had even bought my husband a bottle of it for his birthday when we were dating. It never smelled that great on my husband, but on Parker it mixed well with his chemistry and smelled heavenly.

Many times, Parker and I would hang out at his house. We would talk, drink and smoke cigarettes. Sometimes we would watch tv, but that was rare. I longed to be with him intimately and was frustrated. We would kiss; often we would be kissing, and he would stop, and he would cup my face in his hands and look deep into my eyes as if looking right into my soul. Sometimes I felt as though it was better than having sex.

I was falling in love with Parker. I could tell that he was falling in love with me too. Since he was always drinking, I was the one who would drive us around. We always had to have some good music on the radio. I loved to listen to music in the car with him. Sometimes when I was driving, out of the corner of my eye I would catch him gazing long and hard at me. I felt that he was in love with me. Although, we were falling in love with one another I was also very frustrated with Parker and our relationship. We had been dating for a couple months by then and we had not yet been physically intimate, we didn't go anywhere significant and do things that most couples do. I wanted to go to concerts with him and go camping; I was very disappointed about not doing those things. I was frustrated because I had been feeling all this new-found freedom from leaving my husband and it felt as though I had hit a brick wall of restriction within my relationship with Parker.

    I knew that he was the biggest flirt ever and that he was flirting with and carrying on with other women when he wasn't with me. He was the quintessential stereotypical truck driver. I had thoughts of breaking up with him, and I did try to break up with him and told him he needed to treat me better if he wanted me around. I didn't expect the reaction I got from him. He was very nervously pacing in the kitchen and he seemed like he was pissed off. I sensed he wanted to hit or break something. He said, *"But I love you!"* I think he reactively spoke without realizing what he was saying, because as he was saying it, he caught himself. I was shocked he said this and coupled with his reaction I knew he meant it. Within a couple weeks of Parker telling me that he loved me, he asked me to be his girlfriend. I was good with it, and I thought maybe there was hope that our relationship would go to the next level. We leaned on each other for the past few months during our personal transitions.

    There were times when Parker would tell me I should go back to my husband and try to work things out. Hearing him talk like that would really piss me off but I knew that Parker felt responsible for the breakup of my marriage. At times I thought he might be seeing somebody else and he didn't want to hurt me. I was the one who left, and I never wanted to look back. I was in a far better place without my husband and I don't know how many times I tried to convey to Parker that he was only the catalyst, not the reason. I knew how guilty Parker felt about my marriage crumbling. It wasn't his fault, I never blamed him for it and I always took responsibility for my actions.

Parker was planning on taking some vacation time in October and he wanted to take me to Markleville. He had been there before and stayed in a cabin up there. I was excited and looked forward to going to the mountains and being alone with him for a couple of nights. We had never stayed the night with each other, and we had planned on being intimate. We also planned on fishing and drinking and then drinking some more.

The big vacation week came, and I was working a mobile home deal with a client who didn't mind texting or calling me at three in the morning. My husband and I were negotiating back and forth over our marriage settlement agreement. I had taken him to court earlier in the month for temporary spousal support and I was awarded temporary support. He was pissed off that he had to surprisingly pay me money every month on top of the rent I was collecting from our rentals. My husband was really trying to financially get the upper hand on me with our marriage settlement negotiations. All of it was draining me emotionally. My back hurt and I was exhausted. I was stressed out and really needed this vacation with Parker.

One day before our trip, I was visiting Parker; I think I was on the verge of a nervous breakdown. I don't know why Parker was saying that maybe we shouldn't go on our trip. I burst into tears. I was so frustrated, not only with

Master in the Making

Parker but also with everything else. Parker came to me, put his arm around my shoulder then sat me down and asked what was going on. I said; *"Parker, I am so tired of being jerked around. I need this trip, I am so stressed out. I need to get away. I need a vacation. I need you to promise me that we are going and that we will go for two nights."* He agreed, hugging me. He was so very gentle with me. I felt how much he cared for me in that moment. After all, I was coming undone at the seams.

We went shopping for fishing tackle, and it being a warm Autumn afternoon, we decided to go have a beer at the Dust Bowl. We were planning on having tacos out that night, because it was 'Taco Tuesday' at a place we often frequented, and it was on..., you guessed it; Tuesday!

We were seated across from each other at a table in the bar area, as Parker took a sip of his beer, looked deeply into my eyes, and asked me; *"what do you think about getting married?"* I chuckled. I didn't think he was serious, but then I noticed the disappointed look on his face. I had thought it was a hypothetical question. My jaw dropped. I chose my words carefully and said; *"I'm not even divorced yet!"* I know I must have made him feel a little defeated and hurt, however that was not my intention.

I couldn't believe what had just happened. My head was spinning. I was nervous and really taken aback. I felt like I wanted to run away. I wasn't ready to get married again. I didn't know if I *ever* wanted to get married again. I know that I wasn't ready to marry Parker or anybody else. I loved him, but I wasn't sure that I wanted to continue to be his girlfriend for much longer. There was a part of me that wanted to say yes to Parker's proposal. I did want to be with him, but I wanted more from life than what I was getting from Parker and what I had been through with my husband. I had just ended a twenty-one-year marriage and was trying to find myself and my place in life.

We drank our beer and went outside for a cigarette. I almost left you hanging, readers: I said to him; *"I'm not ready to get married. I would consider living together. How would you feel about living together?"* He didn't like that idea, because we would be living in sin. Odd thing to come out of the mouth of this 'stereotypical bad boy' truck driver.

Parker and I went on our mini vacation to Markleville. It was fall, and being a mix of mountains and high desert, the view looked so serene, with the leaves on the trees turning yellow and red. It was warm for the middle of October; the sun was shining, and it was beautiful out. The place we were staying at was cute. There were about twelve or so old, but well-maintained cabins, each equipped with bathrooms and small kitchens.

When we had planned our trip, I requested that he make reservations for the cabin that had the claw foot tub. There's just something I love about a claw foot tub, maybe because they seem old fashioned and I like taking baths in them. He had gotten the cabin with the claw foot tub for me. I felt special, that he had done that for me.

Parker had been there before, and I had the thought that maybe he had taken someone else there who may have been special to him. I thought that he was wanting to recreate something he had then, with me. Later, I was corrected by Parker. Parker had never taken another woman to Markleville with him. He had only been there to fish with friends and family. I had really thought that he was wanting to recreate something he had before and so that's why I had thought things didn't happen intimately for us. At the time, he said it was a mistake that he took me there and that we should have gone somewhere else. He must have thought that I wasn't having a good time, but I did have a good time, aside from also dealing with a demanding Real Estate client and marriage settlement negotiations with my husband.

I was very disappointed and hurt; my feelings carrying over into the next day. By the way the fishing sucked too. Parker had caught one little itty-bitty trout. We had gone into town to get some alcohol; a fifth of Fireball. Parker asked the store clerk if he knew of any other places to go fishing, he suggested somewhere so we decided we would go and give it a try. It was a little bit of a drive.

When we got there, we found out it was catch and release; and some other restrictions on fishing. We both thought: *This, sucks. Fuck this! Let's go back and fish in the stream.* I was beside myself with this trip; it wasn't turning out the way I had hoped it would. My expectations were not met, and I was thoroughly frustrated. I reminded myself that you can't be disappointed if you don't have expectations and that I was on vacation and I was supposed to be relaxing; so, I said to myself, *"Fuck it, I'm getting fucked up."* I took a couple of swigs of that *fine* cinnamon whiskey. It was so freaking hot out and I had my doc martins on. I was in the passenger seat, so I was able to rip off my socks and shoes. As I laid my seat back, enjoying my buzz, I observed Parker as he slowly drove us back to the cabin. (He had bitched about my driving earlier, so now he was in the driver's seat, realizing what it is like to drive around those curves.)

Master in the Making

We finally arrived back from the bunk fishing lake, I hit the beer and had some more whiskey. I knew Parker wanted to go back out and to fish, but I was exhausted. We'd had wine the night before and the sugar in the wine acted like a stimulant to me, preventing me from getting a good night's sleep; that and the two of us each got up multiple times to go to the bathroom. I never take naps, but that day I did, and it felt good. Parker had gone out to fish but a little while later something woke me up. He was just going back out the door after using the bathroom. I was half asleep but was hoping he would come back in and cuddle with me at least! No chance of that happening. He went fishing again. I was still buzzing. If I put my boots back on and went out walking around and climbing up and down the banks to the stream, I probably would have ended up bloodied and bruised. I sat at the picnic table in the back and drank some more.

My husband had been texting me, wanting to finalize our marriage settlement agreement; I refused to budge, or negotiate with him; what I had asked for was fair and reasonable. Had he taken my initial offer to an attorney they probably would had advised him to sign and run. I was feeling very beat up about it all. Being married to my husband, I knew his tactics; he wanted to wear me down and put pressure on me to get what he wanted. I knew that my husband had an agenda as to why he was being so persistent about our marriage settlement. I thought he might be moving in with his girlfriend or wanting to get remarried. I didn't care about those things, but what I did care about was the pressure, and wanting a fair deal, in writing. I just wanted to be completely done with my husband.

Master in the Making

I was sitting at the picnic table when Parker came back from fishing. I was listening to music and working on real estate paperwork while he was gone. He exclaimed; *"Why didn't you come and find me?"* I responded; *"Because I do not know how to track 'The "Parker" in the wild.' You could have gone in either direction and God only knows how far you had walked in any direction."*

That evening was still uneventful in the way of being physically intimate. I knew Parker had a lot of issues and that's a big reason why it hadn't happened for us. He had medical reasons too. I know too well that it's more of a mental, emotional and medical problem. I too had my own issues. He had been abused sexually, physically, emotionally and mentally as a child. He and his family had been abandoned by his father when he was a young teen. I felt very sympathetic toward him. It's not easy to talk about or express true feelings. Nevertheless, I had expectations, which left me feeling frustrated, disappointed and angry.

Our drive home was quiet. My husband was still texting me while I was driving, so I asked Parker to read the texts to me. One text said that he *did* love me. Parker said; *"he loves you. You should try to work things out with him."* I responded; *"Parker, you don't understand. You don't understand why he is saying these things."*

When Parker told me to work things out with my husband, it pissed me off. my husband and I were going back and forth on our marriage settlement and within two months our divorce would be final. I knew my husband was saying he loved me tying to play my emotions in hopes of it helping him in our negotiations. He was just trying to manipulate me.

Master in the Making

I had seen and heard things like this our entire marriage, he was always trying to be smooth.

When we had first started dating, Parker had asked me to never try to change him. I honored his request, but I *did* want him to change for me. I wanted him to quit his job, quit drinking, and more than anything, I wanted him to stop flirting with anything that moved. I wanted his attention to be focused on me. I wanted to be his 'one and only.' I want to explain that I am not a raving lunatic and not a needy, possessive bitch. I wanted Parker to quit his job to put his skills and talents to use making a living, and I wanted him to quit drinking so that he could think more clearly about everything. He could never give me those things. I never asked him to change. I knew he would resent me and our relationship would never be the same. He would hate me for trying to change him. I just left a twenty-one-year marriage because I was not put as a priority and my husband could never do that for me.

3

Disturbed

    I knew I had to let go of Parker. I was miserable. I didn't want to break up with him, but I had to for me. I was slowly losing my self-respect being with Parker. I was becoming an alcoholic, which I didn't like to see in myself. I wasn't liking myself very much at this point. I was drinking constantly when I was with him and I was compromising my self-respect and wellbeing. I was, in a sense, subconsciously using him to ignore the fact that I needed to work on myself and find myself. I was putting *him* first in my life, and not myself. I had been in this position more than once before, in my life. The only way to change that was to remove myself from the situation, and from the people with whom I surrounded myself. I don't blame him for any of this; I, myself, had made the choices to behave in this way, and I was taking responsibility for me and my actions.

    My heart was breaking. My logical and rational mind knew I should break it off with Parker, but my heart wanted otherwise. I couldn't go on in this relationship because I was constantly being let down. I wanted our relationship to be so much more than this fun-loving friendship. I wanted to see Parker grow and thrive. I wanted to see *myself* grow and thrive. I wanted us to grow and thrive as a couple. I knew Parker wasn't capable of it at that point in time and it was possible that he would never be capable of ever having a relationship like that, whether it was with me, or with anyone else.

As frustrated as I was, I decided to stick around a little longer. The holidays were coming up and it's hard to be alone during that time. I knew it was going to be difficult for me too, and I heard Parker tell me many times that he felt that the holidays were going to be very depressing for him. He and I, both, had loved the holidays when we both had families to share them with. He had loved decorating his home and being festive. I did too. Neither of us were going to have that this year. I didn't want to be alone and I didn't want to break up with him before the holidays. I didn't want to cause him anymore grief than he was already anticipating.

We continued as normal throughout the rest of October. November brought Thanksgiving. I wanted to do a big meal at my apartment for us, but he wouldn't allow me to. I did bake some pies, but that was for me because I needed to bake, and it was the one thing in my life at that time that was therapeutic. I hated cooking, but *baking,* that was cathartic. We ended up at the Sizzler for Thanksgiving Dinner. I hated it, but it *was,* what it was.

In December, I took Parker to my Christmas Party. I got very drunk, very quickly. I can't remember exactly how many shots of liquor I'd had. He didn't dress up for me at all. I thought I deserved that at least. He hit on one of my coworkers and that pissed me off. We ended up leaving when dessert was being served. He knew I was thoroughly pissed by what he had done. It was so disrespectful. He coaxed me to have another drink at the bar. I wanted to go home. It was very cold, windy, and raining. We were in the parking lot and I wanted a cigarette at that point. I was so mad I was shaking. I looked at Parker and his eyes were very big, he knew he had hurt me. He looked scared of me and what I might say to him. He knew I was very disappointed in his behavior. He was trying to put a band aid on my hurt with another drink.

Parker had wanted me to meet his friend Mark and his wife. He was also talking about introducing me to his sister. There was a part of me that really did not want to meet them. Call me crazy, but I felt as though if I did meet them, I would feel even more obligated to continue to date Parker. I wanted to run in the opposite direction. I felt very honored that Parker cared about me and wanted to share me with the people in his life. I agreed to meet his friend Mark, and Mark's wife. A couple of days before New Year's Eve we went to their house, I drank way too much. Parker and Mark put me in bed in a camper on the property. I'm not too sure if I had fallen asleep or not. I don't know how, but I had my phone with me in that camper. I heard a message notification. It was a high school friend of mine who told me that one of our mutual good friends from high school had passed away. I was still drunk and was having a hard time focusing my eyes on this message and then comprehending the message itself. My dear friend, Debbie, had passed away. Not too many months prior, a group of high school friends and I, had attended Debbie's mother's funeral.

This message really shook me. I was having a hard time digesting the fact that my friend who was the same age as me, had died. Debbie and I were thick as thieves in high school. We didn't see much of each other after graduation, but when I had seen Debbie over the years, she didn't seem genuinely happy. There seemed to be this sadness about her that she was trying to cover up. She also seemed to be groggy from medication. I recall her slurring her words a few times. I sensed that she was in pain and carried deep hurt with her.

When death appears in our lives, we tend to look at ourselves in one way or another. For me, I questioned whether I was truly happy in my life. Where I was at and where I was going. The fact was that no I wasn't happy where I was at, and what I was doing. I hadn't been truly happy in a very, very long time.

I didn't want to be alone in that camper any longer. I ventured up the hill to the house. I told Parker that I just learned of my friend passing away and I wanted him to go to the camper with me. He was even more drunk than me. It wasn't a very safe place to be; drunk on a dark hill with brick and concrete steps. I struggled with Parker as he was telling me not to let him fall. He was much bigger and very heavy for me to guide. He was also not steady and stumbling on his own, and I wasn't the greatest of help as I was still drunk and stumbling. I got him back to that camper without having anybody lose blood or consciousness.

I thought the struggle was over, but we still had to deal with the steps into the camper, and then two more up and into the bed. Parker stumbled and grabbed the curtain room divider that hung from the ceiling. I tried to push him onto the bed when I saw him falling but he was too heavy and drunk for me to maneuver; the curtain ripped from the ceiling and Parker fell between the wall and the bed. I don't know for sure, but I am confident he had bruises afterward.

I don't remember how our dialogue began in that camper. I am pretty sure that it was me and that it was about me pleading with Parker to change and commit to our relationship. I told him that I loved him and wanted to be with him. And of course, as usual; Parker telling me that I needed to find somebody else, to find a good man, a rich man, a man that would take care of me like I deserved to be taken care of. This night's dialogue was a little different from those that had preceded; I had never heard Parker talk like he did that night. I had never been around Parker when he was that drunk. To this day I really don't know what he was going through or where he was exactly in his head. What I do know is that Parker was in a very dark place, both emotionally and mentally. "I'm an alcoholic. I'm no good for you. I'm a truck driver that basically makes minimum wage. You need to find somebody better than me."

Although this may have been the truth, it was hard for me to hear him talk so poorly of himself. It was hard for me to listen to him say the truth out loud. I knew all of this, but at the time I didn't care and told him so. I wanted to be with him and wanted a future together with him. I knew that this was my heart talking, but my logic and reasoning told me he was right.

I knew the true Parker, the real Parker underneath all this garbage. I knew underneath the tough alcoholic truck driver veneer lay a very hurt person who covered it up with alcohol and anything else that would divert his attention away from his pain. And beyond all of that there was this truly awesome person. A skilled fisherman, hunter and taxidermist, Parker was also an amateur mycologist, talented drummer, and artist. A nerdy guy who loved to potter around the house, tend to his plants, and put up yard decorations. He was the clown who was always cracking jokes. He liked to cook and was good at it. A kind, gentle, humble and warm, good-hearted man. This is the man I had fallen in love with. He just happened to be a 'stereotypical alcoholic' truck driver.

I had Parker read most of what you have read thus far. He had called me and wanted me to be aware that when he was married to his second wife, she had taken him to a medical center to go into an alcohol treatment program. He claimed that his health at the time was good. He said that through the interview process that the medical center treatment program declared, that he was not eligible for the program because they did not consider him to be an alcoholic. I think I will let you, the reader, decide for yourself.

I saw Parker's potential. Parker, like so many people, including myself, fear facing our fears and pains to live our true potential and to be our authentic selves. It's so much easier and safer to follow the course we grow used to; the rut we live our life in. It's easier to wallow in self-pity and to blame other people for our situation in life. It's easy to not take responsibility for ourselves in one way or another. No one is immune from this. Change is hard. Change requires growth. Change can be painful. I knew that I would never be able to change Parker. Only Parker can change Parker and only if Parker wanted to change. It wasn't my job to change Parker or anybody else.

We both woke up early, feeling like shit, with little sleep and big hangovers. The hour-long drive home was quiet, and it felt like there was a dark cloud hanging over us. It was a little gloomy outside, but I am talking about the atmosphere inside the car. We didn't have much to say to each other. He knew I was disappointed with him. I could see him out of the corner of my eye looking at me with those big brown scared eyes. It was the same look he had at my Christmas Party in the parking lot, a couple of weeks earlier. It was now New Year's Eve. We had plans to go out, but that evening he cancelled on me. I suspected that he had gone out with somebody else that night.

I had already made up my mind to break it off with Parker. I wasn't sure what kind of reaction I would get from him. I thought possibly the truck driver attitude; "fuck you, I was going to break up with you anyways." I was going break up with him on New Year's Day, but New Year's Day came and went. We texted back and forth and had talked on the phone. I didn't really know what was going on with him. The following week I didn't see him at all. I knew that he was more than likely seeing somebody else and I had to just get this breakup over and done with. I was hurting myself by staying in the relationship feeling like this. I didn't really want to break up with him over the phone, but I had to do it for me. It had to be done. I wasn't seeing anybody else. I didn't want to see anybody else. I wanted him, but it just wasn't going to happen the way I wanted it to.

It was the evening of January 8th, 2017 and one of us called the other. I finally blurted out; *"Parker. I didn't want to have to do this over the phone, but you have avoided me all week. I'm sorry, I can't do this anymore. I have to break up with you."* I know I was sobbing. *"I am breaking my own heart. I love you very much. I will always love you."* I was hurting so bad. At the other end of the phone I heard Parker's voice crack, I knew he was on the verge of crying. I was breaking his heart. His reaction felt and sounded very genuine: *"Well, do you think we will ever get back together?"* I responded; *"Parker, I don't know. I just don't know."*

I knew that it would require so much change on his part that it would be almost impossible. He would hold resentment toward me for asking him to change. I knew only too well about waiting around on men to change; after all I had done it for twenty-one years prior. How much more of my life was I going to wait for other people to change? ***I was the one who had to change***, and ***I,*** was the one who had to take the steps toward finding my own happiness. I was heartbroken. I can't really remember how the conversation ended. I don't remember what else was said, but I know we agreed we could still be friends and would meet up for 'Taco Tuesday' every now and then.

Little did I know at that time, what kind of an impact that my relationship with Parker would have on me and my life's purpose. Everything happens for a good reason. I had no idea that God had placed Parker in my life and used him. Later, I would find out that Parker was my soulmate. My breakup with Parker would guide me down a spiritual path that would lead me to a cave in the middle of a desert, in another state, and that I was destined to become a Spiritual Healer and Teacher.

After I broke up with Parker, the two of us tried to be friends. We even hung out together and did our 'Taco Tuesday thing.' He would call me, text me; and I, him. We were the same people, but it seemed like we were even sadder being together knowing we couldn't *'be together'* but knowing we were not together at all. The break up wasn't easy, I loved him very much. I knew it was in my best interest not to date him anymore, but my heart ached for him. I thought about him all the time. I knew his schedule and would think about where he might be and what he might be doing.

There came a point when Parker was texting me and calling me and it hurt. It felt like he was toying with me. You know when you are a kid, and the boy who likes you pulls your ponytail and hurts you? It felt just like that, but it was more painful because this grown ass man couldn't verbally communicate his feelings with me. All he did was tease and taunt me. I guess I would do the same to him in a way; I would text or message him from time to time.

I didn't have that much trouble getting over my ex-husband and I had at one time loved him very much. My husband provided for me and was a good father and husband. Our relationship had lacked in areas and for a while I was angry with my husband. I live by the motto that "everything happens for a reason." Standing back and looking at my life I summed up my marriage as having served its purpose. I didn't hate my husband, nor was I in love with him any longer. I had forgiven my husband in my heart for not being what I wanted and needed. Our marriage wasn't entirely awful or ugly. I saw the biggest blessing as having raised two wonderful boys with this man.

I so wanted Parker to show up on my doorstep just to say Hi. I just wanted to see Parker. It was hard to go places that Parker and I had gone to together. He was constantly on my mind. I had never had such a hard time with a breakup in my life. I couldn't figure out why I was having such a hard time with it. I wondered if it was because I was older, and he was my first boyfriend since before my husband. It had crossed my mind that Parker was my soulmate. I had even told some girlfriends of mine that Parker was my soulmate.

In trying to get over Parker and move on, I decided I would do some online dating. It was exciting but at the same time wore me out. I developed an addiction to checking the dating sites and messages. I did go on a few dates. A select few had the privilege of a second date or more. There was one who was fun to hang out with. He had his issues, and many were too much like Parker's issues, but we still had our fun. A series of embarrassing events occurred, which ended me seeing this one guy. This guy kept asking me if my kids were going to show up and surprise me on Mother's Day. My youngest son, who had a key to my home, *did* come to surprise me on Mother's Day. My son didn't take heed that there was a different car parked in front of my house, and that my car was gone; nor did he try to call or text me before letting himself in. He walked in on this guy in my house and that was the end of that relationship.

I was back on the dating sites once again. It was tiring. It took a lot of energy to message back and forth, trying to decipher how much was true in the dating profiles. I started talking with this good-looking guy. We had some deep conversations. I was sensing that something was off. The phone numbers, locations and information I was getting did not add up and so I asked him to send a photo of his identification. I got some half assed answer, so I called 'bullshit' on this guy. The response I got was *"Ok."* This person wasn't at all the persona that was being portrayed on the online profile, it was completely fake. This act is called 'catfishing.' Unfortunately, I allowed this experience to impact me.

4

Faith No More

I began to feel defeated by life, and by my circumstances. I was at the point where I lost my faith in human beings to be open and honest with each other. I lost my faith in humanity. In losing my faith in humanity, I questioned my faith in God. There was only one other time I can recall when I had lost my faith in God and that was when my blood family of origin broke their promise to help me take care of my Grandparents; I stopped speaking to and interacting with my family five years earlier. At that time, I felt that God had abandoned me and didn't care about me; filled with despair and depressed, I viewed the world in a dark and seedy light. I felt as though my naive and innocent view of the world was shattered, I only saw darkness and ugliness. I had always viewed people as inherently good and that "everything happens for a reason"; I had lost that.

During this time, I had a friend called Devlin; she was my best friend with whom I spoke daily. She tried to help lift my spirits and was there for me when I decided to leave my husband and divorce him. I was there for her when she needed to talk and needed support. Devlin mentioned that she had a friend who does Reiki, which is energy healing. I did a little research on Reiki and decided to sit on the idea as an option; I was giving it some serious thought.

Master in the Making

After my discussion with Devlin about Reiki, I had another one of those dreams; a dream with a message like the one about dying within six months to a year. The message from this dream was for me to give Reiki a lot of thought as it would not be an easy thing to do. The dream focused heavily on the fact that I would see things and learn about myself that I may not want to know, and it may be very emotionally difficult for me to go through. It was an intuitive warning to me to be prepared to endure a difficult period.

I finally decided to contact Devlin's friend, Trisha, through Facebook and told her that I wanted to move forward with doing a Reiki session. Trisha lived in Idaho, so it was decided she would send long distance Reiki. We set up an appointment for nine in the morning. on the Friday of that week. She asked that I believe in a Higher Power. (I was okay with this except I was questioning the strength of my faith. When I was much younger, I had a very strong relationship with God. I wasn't much of a church goer and never belonged to a church. I had more of a one-on-one relationship with God.)

Trisha asked me to also focus on the areas that I wanted healing for the Reiki session. I decided on the depression I was feeling from having lost my faith and seeing the world as cold and dark. I also wanted to get out of the rut I felt my life had been in for years; and to be more focused.

On the Thursday night before my Reiki session I was out eating dinner with my friend Cyndee, when Facebook messenger messages came through on my phone. Firstly, Trisha asked if we could move the time to seven. Then my friend Devlin messaged me and wanted to know if I was going to make an appointment with Trisha to do a Reiki session. I told her yes, I was going to do Reiki. Devlin messaged that she was going to tell Trisha that I wanted to do the Reiki. I sat there shaking my head and thinking to myself "What the fuck? What the fuck is she thinking? I was wondering why she feels that she needs to intervene with me doing this. I was obviously very capable of making an appointment on my own. I felt intruded upon. It felt like my friend was crossing a big line with and it pissed me off. Why was she trying to run my life?" She had overstepped her bounds. I sat there telling Cyndee what was going on and she had the same response I did. I messaged Devlin and told her that I had already made an appointment for the following morning.

There was a good reason for me to be pissed off at Devlin. I had already felt that she had been trying to control me in some ways. She had recently told me that I shouldn't be friends with Cyndee. She also told me that I should unfriend Parker on Facebook and never speak to him again. One day she had come to my house and found it necessary for some reason to tell me that I had clothes in my dryer. She had been getting underneath my skin. The Reiki thing was one more of those things that she was telling me to do. Why was it such a big deal to her to feel that she needed to go this far?

The following morning, on June 2nd, 2017, I had my first Reiki session. I didn't feel anything different at the time. I was doing my morning routine and had a phone conversation with a client. Later in the day I felt tired and worn out. My eyes hurt, and they were burning. Saturday evening, Cyndee and I decided that we would get a manicure and pedicure, then afterwards go have dinner. By the time I got my manicure I was completely exhausted and ready to go to bed at five in the evening. I'm sitting there looking at Cyndee who just spent the day painting her bedroom after having chemotherapy while I was receiving Reiki. I thought that I should have been the one running circles around Cyndee.

Over the course of the next week I was feeling more and more ill. I felt like I was detoxing from heroin (which I have never been addicted to and never done in my life). I was nauseated, had stomach knots and pains, chills, feverish, flushed and I wasn't sleeping well at all. I also felt very empty and lost. I felt like from my stomach up all my feelings and emotions had been stripped from me. I felt like I had even lost my sense of humor.

Devlin called me that weekend and asked how I was feeling. She started telling me that Trisha had done an intuitive reading on me and had told Devlin all about it. I asked more and more questions. Devlin answered but when I went deeper and deeper into my questioning, she suddenly became confused about what Trisha had said, and suddenly forget what was said. *Why would Trisha tell Devlin about my Intuitive reading and not me?* After all, it was *my* Reiki session that she did the intuitive reading on. I intuitively knew that Devlin was keeping something from me.

Devlin told me that I needed to get over my trust issues, depression and anxiety or whatever that was. She told me that I was going to need to have many more Reiki sessions. She asked me if I had visions or heard angelic voices. She told me that I needed to talk to my mom or a psychiatrist or psychologist, because I was going to need one. I told her NO! Why did I tell her no? Well, there again she was trying to tell me what to do. How would *she* know if I had depression, trust issues and anxiety? I don't believe I had ever displayed these things to her or others? Why would she tell me to talk to my mom, with whom I hadn't spoken with in five years? Why would I need a psychiatrist or psychologist? Why would she say such things to me without an explanation? Was she trying to be mean? Was she really trying to help me? Why would I need to seek mental help? What did she know that I didn't know? Why did she feel the need to tell me that I needed to get over my depression, anxiety and trust issues? Was that something that was in my intuitive reading? I had never been diagnosed with any issues. I knew that I was little depressed with my view of the world and losing my faith in humanity. I had just gone through a divorce and broke up with a boyfriend, and then I was catfished. I had a lot anxiety through all of that, but ongoing depression and anxiety was not an issue for me.

I'd had it with Devlin. A couple of days later I saw her at our monthly Bunco, and she came up to me and asked me how I was feeling. I was feeling like crap and had since the Reiki. I was starting to wake up at three in the morning. I was exhausted, felt lost and very empty. I was angry with her and at this point didn't trust her. She looked me straight in the eyes with this weird 'shit eating' grin on her face and told me that I was going to be just fine and that I was going to feel so much better. Of course, again, I am thinking; *what the fuck does she know?* I am a grown ass adult who knows that I am going to be just fine and that I would feel better sooner or later.

Master in the Making

    The day after our meeting at Bunco, I woke up intuitively knowing, with every fiber of my being, that Devlin was absolutely keeping something from me. I was angry. Every inch of my body was shaking from the rage I felt toward Devlin and Trisha, because by this time I also felt that they both had done something that they shouldn't have done involving my Reiki session. I wanted to hit something, but I couldn't as I had to tend to the business of showing a client a property. This client was not an easy client to help find a home, which seems to be the case with all first-time home buyers. I was out with this client, leaving one property and in the processes of going to the next home. I knew exactly where the next property was, but was so out of it with the rage that I was feeling that I thought it would be best if I put the address in my navigation app. In the past I have had my phone act up when I was excited. In the past it was when I was helping another client crunch the numbers on payments. This time it was a little different. I was very angry. If you had seen me, I probably looked like one of those cartoon characters that turns red and has steam coming out of their ears. This time my phone navigation app was trying to take me in a circle back to where I had started from. That was a crazy experience that left an impression on me.

    If *that* wasn't weird, the following day I was working in the yard. I had been outside for some time and when I came inside my phone lit up, then my computer lit up. I did not have any notifications or messages coming in, on either! I noted it as strange. Then I had been charging a power tool battery and when I went to unplug the charger it stayed lit for more than a minute. Some people may not look at this as anything significant, but I took this as my angels were trying to tell me something; they were trying to tell me I was right about Devlin and Trisha.

I have had things like this happen to me before. Years ago, when I lived in South Lake Tahoe and worked at Bass shoes, I had been speaking to my mother on the phone about my trip back home to visit. I told her I would just talk to her when I saw her. I was the only person in the store, and I hadn't opened the store yet. I went to use the restroom. While I was in the restroom a clipboard fell off the wall and there was no way for it to just fall off the wall. I started to feel very nervous and had an intuitive gut feeling. I sensed that something was going to happen that day and it had something to do with my mother.

I called my mother back and told her that I wasn't going to call her again, but I think that something is going to happen today and that I think it is something to do with her. I asked if she would call me back if something significant happens. I want to say within three hours my mother called me back and told me that my half-sister, Tara had called her. This was very significant, as my mother had put my sister up for adoption when she was born and had never had contact with her since. My sister found her biological mother.

So, I guess you can say that I have some sort of Spidey sense, or senses. Around the same time, I had been living in Tahoe I had a roommate, Stacey. She was out of town working during the week and would be home on the weekends. I had been gone a lot too, as I would often go and stay with my boyfriend down in Carson City. One evening, I felt a presence that I had felt before when I was in my apartment; it was a little unnerving. I felt uncomfortable because I felt like I was being watched. I finally asked Stacey if she felt a presence. I didn't expect to get the answer I got. Stacey proceeded to tell me that she'd had this presence you can call a ghost or spirit with her since she was a little girl.

My point in telling you my past occurrences is that I have had these types of intuitive experiences in the past. This time my Spidey senses had been telling me that Devlin and Trisha had, in fact, done me wrong. It wasn't just that Trisha and Devlin had a conversation about me that Trisha had shared my intuitive reading with Devlin; or that Trisha and Devlin refused to tell me everything about the intuitive reading. Intuitively, I felt that there was something beyond all those things. I sensed that they had done something else and it wasn't my will or God's will; it was their will upon me. Since this I have become a Reiki Master and I know that in doing Reiki on somebody you always have the best and highest intentions for the client. Even if you love the person and have an interest in seeing them heal, you NEVER put your own intentions into the Reiki. This is something I have been very cautious about when dealing with clients; it's always for their best and highest good. I considered this as a form of 'ego' when a healer puts their own intentions into a healing session.

That weekend I messaged back and forth with Devlin many times. I had messaged Trisha as well about the conversation between her and Devlin. I asked Trisha about my intuitive reading and asked why she wouldn't share it with me. She and Devlin held to the reason being it was just a conversation between two girlfriends. Devlin would argue over terminology and words I was using when I was asking her questions about what Trisha had picked up in my intuitive reading. I wasn't getting the answers I was seeking from either of them. I'd had it with Devlin. This was the straw that broke the camel's back for me. I decided that I would just cut her out of my life and I blocked her on Facebook and on my phone.

Little did I know that Devlin had a couple more Facebook accounts. When she realized that I had blocked her, she used another one of these accounts to contact me. She wanted to have her say. She wanted me to know that she felt that she was giving her whole self to help me heal. She said she had taken time from herself and others to help me. This was a surprise to me. I didn't see things the same way Devlin had. I really thought that our friendship was a give and take. She felt that our relationship was very one sided and that I was doing all the taking in the relationship. If she didn't have time to talk with me or spend time with me, I would have understood. The thing is Devlin never once expressed to me that she had to tend to other things at all, but now I was receiving all this backlash from her. Devlin also expressed that she felt that I wasn't appreciative of Trisha doing Reiki for me. Devlin had told me Trisha had her own problems and was very busy, but she took time out to do my Reiki. I really would have understood if Trisha didn't have the time or energy to do a Reiki session for me. I wasn't pushing or pressing Trisha or Devlin for a Reiki session. I had waited to do it for two months anyhow. I wasn't in a big hurry. Waiting a little longer wouldn't have mattered to me and there were other people in my area who did Reiki.

Devlin went on to tell me she had been having nightmares that I was trying to destroy her, that she was sick to her stomach and that she couldn't eat or sleep. I found it interesting that those were the exact same symptoms that I had been feeling with my detox. I didn't have any nightmares. I found it very odd that Devlin was having these symptoms. Sure, she was very upset with me as I was with her, but the thing is that Devlin was an empath and had other psychic abilities.

Devlin had recently told me that she thought I had ghosts in my office. Why would she know this and even bring it up with me? Why would she pick these things up? Was she trying to pick things up about me and why? It made me feel uncomfortable. She had only been in my office once to pick up a key. At one time I had thought there might have been a ghost in my office too. I never really got that usual intuitive Spidey sense of a ghost though, it was more of an eerie feeling when in a big space by yourself. There were a couple of doors that would rattle, but I concluded that it was the wind and not a ghost.

Devlin shared with me that she was personally working with Trisha on grief she hadn't processed from the loss of one of her brothers. She said that she had not allowed the cord between her brother and herself to be cut when he passed and that she had recently cut that cord and felt much better letting go. When we have relationships with other people, places, and situations, cords are created and attached organically and naturally by our energies. In Devlin's case with her brother, she never allowed that cord to be detached. Normally when somebody passes the cords are cut, because the deceased goes into another plane of existence different than ours here on Earth. Devlin never allowed it to happen, she held on as though her brother was still alive.

I was reeling from Devlin's and Trisha's behavior. I was livid, because I felt violated. I felt I had just had my soul fucked with. An intuitive reading is something I see as more private than my medical file. I didn't sign a HIPPA form, but the information Trisha shared with Devlin was more private than what's covered in a HIPPA form. I felt that these two spiritually abused me. I felt as though it added one more thing to the list of things I had to heal from.

I have recently taken Reflexology and Sacral Cranial Therapy courses. In those courses we had discussed how it isn't necessary to apply a great deal of pressure. If you apply too much force on the body, the body can resist the pressure which can result in an injury. It's not just the body that resists when something is forced upon it; the soul responds in the same way. They didn't think anything was wrong with what they did. What was the motive? Did they have an agenda? What were they hiding from me?

That was it between me and Devlin. I didn't need a friend like her. She had been making me feel bad about myself. She thought she knew what was best for me. She wanted me to live my life according to her. I couldn't, and I will never live my life according to somebody else. Although, I wasn't going to live my life according to her I decided to reach out to my mother and Parker to see if there was any validity in what Devlin was telling me.

I wrote my mother a letter. After I read it through it turned out to be about trust. It wasn't my intention, but I suppose subconsciously that is how I was feeling about my relationship with my mother. I felt she didn't trust me. It didn't make sense when I had written the letter, but it makes a lot more sense now. I also wrote Parker a long text message and told him that he had really hurt me. He had not only attacked me professionally as a real estate agent, but he had attacked me personally. He had attacked my integrity and honesty.

Parker had texted me a month prior saying that I sold him a piece of shit and that I knew it. He was insinuating that I had sold him a piece of shit intentionally. I had called him up right after that text and let him have it. I told him that he needed to take responsibility for his decision and that I thought he knew me better than that. He knew he was wrong for doing that to me. I was only a real estate agent. Inspections were out of my scope of knowledge. I wasn't trained as an inspector. He had refused to get any inspections when he bought it. It felt good to stand up for myself, but then I heard Parker at the end of the phone, and he was speechless. It was Parker pulling my ponytail again. I had never spoken to him like that. I felt bad for him, but in my opinion one of Parker's problems in life is not taking responsibility for his own actions and blaming other people for his position in life.

My insomnia was getting worse. All week I searched the internet for any possible answers about Reiki going wrong, empaths and energy vampires. I was convinced by my research that Devlin was an energy vampire. I wasn't so sure I was an energy vampire or not. When I would go into work during this time, I would try to avoid contact with other people for fear that I was sucking their energy or that they might suck my energy. I was researching energy vampires. Part of me didn't feel comfortable with researching energy vampires, it's a bit crazy. Knowing that Devlin was an empath and that she had made comments about my office having a ghost, I wasn't sure about Devlin's abilities and her motives. I was sensing that Devlin been able to intuitively tap into my feelings and thoughts. And that sounds even crazier, but that's what I felt was going on.

I lit sage and performed rituals to clear my house of Devlin's energy, any negative energy. I blessed and protected my home and myself. A few days after I had 'cleared' my home I felt a presence outside my front door. The security screen door rattled. I got the impression that this was Devlin. She was wanting to get into my space, and she was pissed off that she couldn't come in. I think she rattled the door to scare me. There was no logical or rational reason for that door to rattle the way it did. It was the middle of the summer. I have two security screen doors, one on the front door and one on the backdoor. These doors had never rattled like that. Since then I have paid close attention to these doors and they have never rattled even when there were high winds.

I started searching the internet for cord cutting like Devlin told me she had to do with her brother. I was learning a lot about spiritual stuff on the internet. I felt that I needed to cut the cord with her. I was doing ritual after ritual of cord cutting. Nothing seemed to be working. I felt she was using her intuitive gifts to see what I was doing. I had no idea how to protect myself. I decided that I was going to put Devlin in a big clear bouncy ball in my mind. Whenever I felt her presence come near me, I would imagine that I hit this ball with both of my hands and that she was sent back to where she came from. This seemed to work for me, after a few weeks I stopped feeling her presence around me.

I have known about energy vampires for a while, but I read more in depth about them in my research. Most people have encountered these people but may not know what they are called. An energy vampire is essentially somebody that sucks the energy out of you. You probably have been around an energy vampire before. Think about it. Have you ever felt really drained of energy after having been around somebody? One minute you feel all energetic and then after being with them you feel like you need to take a nap.

Three weeks after my Reiki session, I still wasn't feeling myself. I knew that whatever was wrong with me wasn't a physical illness like a cold, flu or allergies. I knew a medical doctor couldn't prescribe anything that would treat what I was sick with. I would entertain taking a trip to the doctor's office just to rule out any medical issue. I believed that whatever was wrong with me was something spiritual. I knew that it had everything to do with what Devlin and Trisha did. I went to have a chakra healing and balancing done by Lyn Ross, a local woman who I had thought about going to initially and instead of going to Trisha.

Upon meeting Lyn in the front of her shop, I told her that I thought that there was something spiritually wrong with me. She looked me in the eyes, and I knew she could see what was going on with me. Lyn took me to one of her session rooms. It was dimly lit. Light beige linen curtains hung from the ceiling creating a divider between areas of the room. As I walked in, a chaise lounge with an afghan on it was right in front of me. Beyond the curtains, a massage table sat in the middle of the room and there was a buffet with shelving where essential oils and crystals lined the shelves against the wall. A picture of Buddha hung on the wall and a statue of Ganesh on the floor. A small table with a lamp and two chairs sat in the corner near the window.

Master in the Making

Lyn sat me down in one of the chairs. She wanted to chat with me a little bit before she started the healing session. She told me about her background in healing. She asked if I had ever heard of an energy vampire and I nodded and said yes. She told me nothing will shock her, she had seen it a lot as a healer. She has seen people levitate, the table levitate and relatives from the other side come watch and wave. I was still skeptical of the supernatural. I was skeptical as to how this chakra healing and balancing could help me. I didn't know what to expect. I didn't ask any questions. I just wanted to feel better. I wanted my sense of humor back and I didn't want to feel crappy anymore. She told me that she was going to write things down as she worked on me and I agreed to it.

I laid down on the table and was given headphones to put on. Lyn placed a piece of muslin fabric over my eyes and had used an essential oil for aromatherapy. She told me she was going to put on a guided meditation for me to listen to. I began to cry. I had no idea why I was crying. The meditation was focusing on one chakra at a time. A couple of minutes before the meditation would move from one chakra to the next, I felt an internal surge of movement; like a guttural wave. It was as though my mind and body knew or anticipated the switch and reacted to it before it happened. I was still not completely convinced of this hocus pocus stuff and if it would work for me. At one point I had peeked from underneath the fabric over my eyes to the left of me. It looked like the door was open and I saw a ladder in the hallway. Did Lyn have to get the ladder, because I levitated? I wasn't at all sure of what was going on. A few minutes later I looked downward. I was taken aback by what I saw. I was seeing this with my own two sober eyes; Lyn had this radiant blue light illuminating and emanating from her hands and was working on my stomach area. At that point I knew it wasn't 'hocus pocus.' I closed my eyes and went back to the meditation.

When the guided meditation had reached the final chakra, Lyn quietly but sternly said, *"Julie, we are almost done."* I had been concentrating on the meditation and felt a little out of it. As I was becoming more aware of what was going on in the room, it felt like the table was being set on the floor, or that two corners of the table had been kicked. Did I really want to know if I levitated the table? No, not really. What does that mean anyway? What does it mean to levitate a table? Did I really need to know? Did I just see a ladder in the hallway? Blue light coming from this lady's hands? The sensation of a guttural wave surge within me?

Lyn asked me if I felt anything. I told her that my feet tingled. I felt like a weight had been lifted off me. I don't think I was completely telling her the truth and I think she had picked up on that. I had an 'aha' moment as I was editing this; I get it now. I think Lyn was referring to the guttural wave surging in my body. It was an intuitive reaction my mind and body had to the guided meditation she was asking about.

As I climbed down from the table, I felt groggy. I can't remember where I was if I was standing or sitting in the chair by the window again. I remember Lyn going over the things she had written down. The page was filled with different things. These are only some of the things we spoke about. She said that I was very intuitive and that I didn't listen to my intuition. I had suffered a relationship loss. I suffered from a lot of loss and grief. I had much sadness and childhood pain. I didn't have much self-esteem. And I didn't speak my truth.

The one thing she asked me about was if I remember any specific childhood trauma. I quickly thought about it. I thought about a recurring memory of my mother's father doing something sexual to me which I had never thought of as being true; then there was the death of my Great Grandfather Larry and not being able to go to his funeral; and then my first spiritual experience. I settled on sharing my first spiritual experience as it happened when I was somewhere between six and eight years old and it was somewhat traumatizing. Once I told her of the spiritual experience, Lyn asked more questions. Where did this happen and is the house still standing? It happened here in Modesto, in fact my entire original family currently lived in the house. When I told her these things, I sensed that she was very disgusted and sickened that the house still existed and that my entire family still lived there. This led me to believe that the childhood trauma I shared with her wasn't the one she was referring to.

I am pretty sure that Lyn didn't buy the spiritual trauma experience. She said that it would come to me in the next couple of days. I felt nervous and unsettled. I just wanted to run out of the place, but I had to maintain my composure and pay for my session. Lyn very kindly offered to make me a copy of what she had written down in the session. While I waited, I checked my phone for any calls or messages. The first contact in over five years, my mother, had called me and left a voicemail. She had received my letter. She said to call her when I had time.

Master in the Making

I left Lyn's, unsure if this healing would help me or not. I did not know what to expect. I knew that this was a very different healing experience from that of my Reiki experience. I felt more confident that I had come away with a piece of paper with these things written down. I had some point of reference of what I needed to work on. I knew I had to work on 'those things;' whereas my Reiki experience seemed tainted and unfulfilling. This experience had given me some validation that spiritual healers could share their intuitive findings with their patients.

During the days following my chakra healing and balancing, I was still waking up at 3am and was struggling with exhaustion. However, I noticed a significant change at bedtime. In the past I would go to bed with such pain in my heart that I would cry myself to sleep nearly every night. The heavy sadness in my heart had lifted and I was no longer crying myself to sleep.

The same day that I had the chakra healing and balancing I had called my mother back and we talked for a short time. Sunday was Father's Day and I asked if it would be okay if I came to visit then. As I had mentioned prior, I hadn't spoken to my family in about five years. I didn't know what to expect. I did miss them very much. I missed having my family of origin. For years I had hated hearing other people tell me that I should talk to my family, that I should talk to my mother and father because they gave me life. Other people were giving me a guilt trip about not talking with my family. I had already had a guilt trip over it and by other people saying something to me – it was insult to injury. People didn't understand what happened and when I tried to explain their reaction was that it doesn't matter. I had always second guessed myself over my decision to no longer speak with my family. You know, the 'normal' or 'prescribed' roles that are placed on us by society – how we should feel, think and behave.

Just as Lyn had said I would recall the traumatic childhood memory and that more would come; it was that horrible memory that I wasn't giving any truth to. The memory of possibly being sexually abused by my Grandfather while on a trip to visit my mother's family in Canada. I was in the process of recalling little flashes of memory and was able to piece them together.

When I was able to remember how I felt after he had abused me. I was able to see my three-year-old self crying hysterically on the floor of his office and then in his car. I remember not having my underwear and not being able to cover my butt. I didn't want anybody to see my butt. I wanted my underwear. I was wearing a dress and felt exposed.

I know as an adult that my three-year-old self wanted to cover up the shame, guilt and horrific thing that had just happened to me. As I was in my Grandfathers car pleading to have my underwear back, he was insisting I believe and say that I had peed my pants. I remember something running wet coming from my bottom and running down my legs. It wasn't pee. I wasn't going along with what my Grandfather was saying. Him telling me to lie, made what had just happened to me that much more traumatic. As an adult, I was finally able to tie my emotions to the flashback memory I had for years. I was able to accept that this recurring flash of memory *had* happened to me. I was still having a hard time coming to terms with it. I was having trouble accepting the fact that I had repressed memories. I never believed that repressed memories were possible.

Father's Day was on my doorstep. I had to work the morning shift answering the phones and the woman covering the afternoon shift had arrived early. I asked if she would mind if I left early, because I was going to visit my family for the first time in five years. She agreed. I called my mother to see if it was okay to come a little earlier. I was nervous, excited and apprehensive about seeing my family. I knew that my brother, Steven, would probably not speak to me at all, if he was around. I suspected that my father was still holding an undue grudge toward me. My Grandparents had chosen me to act on their behalf as their attorney-at-fact, trustee and executrix, rather than my father.

5

Our House

    Here I stood, in the driveway of my Grandparents house, where my mother, father, brothers and sister-in-law now lived. The gray sided and red brick two-story house with the half circle driveway sat in a small, older subdivision in a semi-rural area of custom homes situated on one-acre parcels. My Grandparents and Great Grandparents had the house built in 1968 and was completed shortly after I was born. So many holidays and memories were from this place. This house held a lot of pain for me as well; pain I felt from my family breaking their promise. In 2008 I was looking to put my Grandparents into a rest home. My whole family had rejected the idea. I had agreed not to put my Grandparents into a home, and they had all agreed to help me take care of my Grandparents.

    This is the house where I had the first most memorable spiritual experience of my life. As mentioned previously, I was between the ages of six and eight. I was staying with my Grandparents and my Great Grandmother, as my parents had gone somewhere and left me and my brothers in their care for a weekend or week. Typically, it was the case that all three of us kids would sleep together in the 'magic bed' in the downstairs family room. The 'magic bed' was a sofa bed. My Grandfather Rudy would play with

Master in the Making

us kids in a game he called the 'scissors.' Rudy was tall and had long legs, he would get us in the clutches of his legs and squeeze us. It was our thing. For some reason, on this stay I was put upstairs in what used to be my Great Grandfather Larry's bedroom. He too was a big tall man and his bed was so big and lonely. I couldn't sleep, and I was scared. My Great Grandmother Gladys was fast asleep in her own room in her own bed.

    I was the only one up in the house. I didn't want to wake anybody. I was feeling nervous, uneasy and afraid. My heart was racing, and my palms were sweating. The room felt cold and eerie. I had turned on the lights in the bedroom, hallway and bathroom. I was standing in the bedroom near the closet and the bedroom door. I physically felt a coldness and as if somebody very big had hugged me. I didn't know what I had just experienced, but at that age it freaked me out. I stayed up all night long that night. I had gone downstairs and waited and waited for my brothers to wake up. I may have woken them up about the time the sun was coming up. I probably rattled on and on to my brothers about what I had experienced. I probably didn't even think about telling my Grandparents, since in my short life I knew that if I told of the things that happened to me the adults wouldn't believe me.

    A part of me thought that this was my Great Grandfather Larry, who had passed away when I was five. We had driven to the hospital in Ceres from Fair Oaks, in my dad's canary yellow 911 Porsche with the three of us kids in the backseat. He was on the verge of passing away. In the car was talk of the impending funeral. I wanted to go to the funeral, but my Grandmother Marjorie had already made it clear that there were not to be any children attending. We went into the hospital room and there he was in the hospital bed. I could see he was very tired, and he looked into my eyes. We were saying goodbye with a look. A lot of people I have discussed death with, talk about how when people are dying, they often wait to die until either somebody arrives to say goodbye, or when their loved ones have left the room. In this case, I believe that my Great Grandfather waited for my father to come and say goodbye. My dad was raised by my Great Grandparents for a little while when he was very young. My Great Grandfather and my dad had a special bond. Almost instantaneously after we had left the room, my Great Grandfather passed away.

    Throughout my life I would pick up on a presence in that room and I knew it was Larry. When my Grandmother was dying in the very same house, I felt Larry was in the downstairs living room. I would call out to Larry and tell him that a light portal was going to be opening and that he should go with her when she passed away. She passed away, but his presence remained. I had no idea why he stayed. After Rudy passed, we were remodeling the house. Alex was in Larry's old room working. Alex was fifteen and when he came out of that room, I knew by the look on his face he was freaked out. He told me he felt something creepy in there and it scared him. I think I laughed out loud. I calmly asked him if what he was feeling was in the entire room or was it only in a certain spot. He said it was a certain spot, so I asked him to show me exactly where he was working. He was reluctant to go back into the room, but I was able to get him to show me where the spot was.

Master in the Making

It was the very same spot where I had stood when I had my first encounter with Larry from the other side. I had never told my children about my experiences in that room, or that I had the ability to sense ghosts. It didn't help Alex to feel any more comfortable about working in that room, in fact it probably freaked him out even more. I tried to do the work in that room myself. The plywood subflooring was exposed and there were some stains on the wood that I couldn't determine if it was blood or wood stain. The house had been built at a time when cabinetry was built on site. I was feeling uneasy about this presence and debating whether it had been Larry at all. The land that the house was built on had been part of the McHenry property at the turn of the century. The McHenry family were a very prominent family, who owned many acres where they had a chicken farm. The original McHenry house still stands nearby my Grandparents home. I thought that maybe something heinous had happened on the land prior and that I was picking up some other presence and not that of my Larry. In my head I had a few conversations with these presences and banished them, along with any others, from the property. I had a few conversations with them asking them to leave; finally, within a couple of weeks, I felt that they were gone.

6
Tell Me Something Good

I felt that I was warmly received by my mother and my brother Greg, but when I saw my dad, he refused my presence. I could tell by his body language and facial expression that he was angry with me. I was so hurt that he didn't come to greet me with a hug and kind words; but then again, I did anticipate some resistance from him. And it's not my dad's style to be a hugger or kisser anyhow, that's just not how my dad rolls. Although I wished my dad was the kind of dad who I wanted and needed in my mind. I used to give Parker shit over him not reaching out to his own kids and trying to have a relationship with them. He had five children; the eldest was thirty-five and the youngest, seven. He had expressed that he loved them all very, very much; but none of them wanted anything to do with him. Now I realize that I was saying this, because this is what I wanted from my own dad. I also realized that when I dated Parker, I was essentially dating my dad.

I went to my parents' house with a Father's Day card in hand. All I could do was leave him alone and lay the card on the counter where he sits. I had prepared myself mentally and had even gone with a list of things to talk about. I had wanted to have my dad present to cover those things, but it didn't happen. The main thing I had wanted to cover was what had happened to me when I was three. I had expressed to my mother prior to my visit that I had something that I needed to talk with her about. I sat and talked with my mother and my brother Greg. I had caught them up about my divorce, kids and life. I spoke of all spiritual things that I had just been through. It left one last thing to talk about and that was the sexual abuse. I had really wanted to be clear that the repressed memory was not something that had been fabricated by me or planted in my mind by anybody else.

    I kept telling my mother that it was something that she didn't want to hear, so I had her on the edge of her seat in anticipation. I didn't know what kind of response I would get from her. I couldn't keep her or myself in suspense any longer, so I told her that I had this recurring memory for a very long time and that I never believed in repressed memories. Then I told her about my memory and the emotions I was able to tie to the event. She seemed stunned, but at the same time it didn't seem to surprise her very much. She felt that she had to tell me again about a family trip to a relative's farm in Switzerland.

    She was four years old and she had an older sister and brother as well as a younger sister. My Grandfather and Grandmother had sat them down and the four of them were being questioned about if anybody had touched them inappropriately. They all said they had not been touched. My mother indicated that there was another little girl on this farm and that she may have been touched, because the following morning a farm hand had been fired. I had heard her tell this story before, but now I wondered why she would ever tell me or anybody this story. Was it that she had suspected her father of touching that little girl? Did my mother have lingering questions in her own mind about who her father was? Was it that she knew what had happened to that little girl and she blocked it out of her mind?

I continued telling my mother what had happened to me beyond the sexual abuse in my Grandfather's office. My Grandfather was driving me to meet my Mother, brothers and some other family members at the Lake. I was still hysterically crying, most likely red-faced and with snot and slobber all over my face. At this point I didn't have much more memory than that to tell her about.

I was still at my parents' house, and my dad had begun to warm up to me in a sense. He spoke to me and asked me about what had happened to my Grandparents belongings. I felt he implied that I had taken everything for myself or that I sold everything and kept the proceeds for myself. I had anticipated this. It was the furthest thing from the truth. I explained that there was only one thing I kept for myself and it only meant something to me and nobody else.

I kept a small two-inch by three-inch silver trinket box that had a small rubber key for lifting glass table tops from furniture. It was my Great Grandmothers. She had kept it on the coffee table since I was young. It was like a childhood toy to me. I remember playing with it, and the suction sound it would make as I lifted it off the glass. Sometimes I was very successful in annoying my Great Grandmother and she'd tell me to knock it off.

Master in the Making

The rest of the things that belonged to my Grandparents had been sold or given away. The proceeds were used to remodel the house. Anything else that I couldn't sell was given to charity. I had no use for any of it. The thing is I didn't just move forward with getting rid of things without first making my entire family aware of what I was doing, and secondly, I had invited every single family member out to the house to take anything that they wanted. Nobody had made a move to come and get anything that they wanted. I couldn't wait for them forever, I had to move forward. I felt I was the only responsible one out of the bunch. Maybe more accurately, I was the one who stepped up and did the work. I needed that chapter of taking care of my Grandparents and anything attached to them over with.

My dad's questions upset me. I knew my family didn't really know me or who I was. I began crying and went to collect my things. I was ready to leave. I promised myself that I wouldn't allow my family to make me feel badly about what I had done. I wasn't going to allow them to think that I had ill intentions or that I was being deceitful and greedy. They always seemed to be able to make me question myself and make me feel bad when I had absolutely no reason to. This was almost like my dealings with my ex-husband's family. I always had my heart and intentions in the right place, but everything I did or said would be twisted in a negative way. My own family didn't trust me or believe what I had to say. My dad saw me upset and realized I was going to leave. He started talking to me differently and walked toward the front door, so I wouldn't leave.

My mother and brother Greg had been outside while I talked to my dad. They were coming in as my dad and I were in the kitchen talking. Not sure how the subject came up, possibly my mother, but it was brought up what I had told her earlier about being sexually abused by my Grandfather in Canada. I continued to tell the story to my dad. I wanted him to know that I had the flash of memories and that I couldn't remember the actual act, because I had blocked it out. I had no idea what to expect when you tell your parents that you have repressed memories of being sexually abused when you were three. I was forty-seven years old and this was all new information, not only to them, but strangely enough it was news to me. I do think my dad was concerned about me, but what stuck in my mind after telling him was that he said he knew something was off about my Grandfather. He wanted my mom to call her childhood friend Suzie. I thought it was an odd reaction. My dad wasn't on that trip to Canada with us. He must have picked up some odd behavior from my Grandfather at some point and had shared his impressions with my mother at some earlier point in time. Mind you, my dad had only been around my mother's parents on less than five occasions. It was time for me to go home after this long emotional day.

7

Pieces

The following week, I tried to listen to guided meditations as Lyn had suggested. At this time, you would often find me at three in the morning drinking coffee, smoking cigarette after cigarette, journaling, or just sitting and thinking on my back patio. I had been talking with my brother Greg, whom had also been learning more about the metaphysical world and spirituality. I had shared my Reiki experience and my Chakra healing and balancing with Greg and mother. I was still very angry over what had happened with Devlin and Trisha, which I also shared. I was still trying to figure out what they did to me and what exactly they hadn't told me. Greg suggested I write a book about my experiences. My mom's side of the family and I had always talked about paranormal stuff and we all knew who Edgar Cayce was. When my Aunt visited, or we visited her in Canada, she always shared paranormal stories. My Aunt had a past life regression done years ago and she had found out that she had been a school teacher in Atlantis. Her stories always fascinated me. My mother would say that her mother was also spiritually gifted. I didn't know my mother's mother very well. I never got the impression she was spiritually gifted. My brother Greg claimed he could see ghosts. I couldn't see ghosts. I could only feel their presence.

Master in the Making

It was interesting that Greg had been on a spiritual journey and been watching a lot of the Gaia channel and YouTube videos. He knew a lot of what I was talking about; like chakras, healing and the dark side. He knew of spirit guides and angels. He was more interested in extraterrestrials, conspiracy theories and the impacts of chemtrails. None of that interested me. I was on a spiritual journey and would explain that I am only focused on locally not globally. Greg had suggested that there were energies that were waking me up and that these energies were spirit guides. After not having been around Greg in the past five years I had a hard time giving credence to what he was saying to me. Later that evening, I searched the internet for information on what I was experiencing, what a spirit guide is, anything of a spiritual nature, and anything connected. I couldn't take what Greg was saying as the gospel.

I was so tired from the lack of sleep. I was waking up drenched in sweat and it wasn't from hot flashes. In late December of 2016 I had moved into one of the rentals I had gotten in the divorce. My house had central heat and air conditioning, so it was nice and cool. I attributed this sweating to detoxing. I was suffering from bloodshot eyes and blurry vision. I wasn't feeling all that great. I felt like I was coming down with something. I was having pressure headaches that seemed to be right across my brow; they didn't cause me pain, but it was uncomfortable from the pressure. Sometimes the pressure seemed like a swirling mass. The only way I can explain this swirling mass is if you have ever seen the movie "Flubber" with Robin Williams. The flubber would move a certain way and that's how the pressure in my forehead and brow would move. I was trying to take better care of myself by allowing myself to stay put and sit on the couch all day if I wanted to. I was constantly crying. It seemed like there wasn't a day or hour that would go by without me crying for six consecutive weeks. I was a wreck. Friends told me I should keep myself busy and work more. I didn't agree with this, because that's exactly what I had been doing all my life, just plowing through and moving on. I figured that I had never made time or space and allowed myself to properly grieve my grandparents, Parker and the other relationship losses in my life.

I was beginning to put some pieces of the puzzle together about Devlin. Devlin didn't want me to hang out with Cyndee or Parker. The whole weird thing with my clothes in my dryer. Devlin had once helped me fold my clothes. When she folded my jeans, she was overly excited and asked what size jeans they were. I told her, but she didn't believe me. She said, *"Oh, these are small."* It was some odd behavior to me. It wasn't so much about the size of the jeans as it was about her behavior. It was like she was getting a thrill out of touching my clothes. There were times I thought Devlin was jealous of me. Sometimes I even thought, she wanted to be me. I was still going over why would Devlin lash out at me like she had. What was her big payoff? What was she going to get out of me having Reiki? I saw us as just being friends. I believed she felt that she had moved mountains to help me. This is when the wheels and cogs lined up for me and it crossed my mind that Devlin was in love with me. Her big payoff was to have my undying love and gratitude. It was unsettling that this long- time friend of mine had been in love with me and never said anything to me about it. I didn't have a clue that she was in love with me.

I recalled that she had brought me some used clothes a couple of months back. I found it odd that she had brought me some clothes. I had thoughts that maybe Devlin practiced magic I had no idea about and that maybe she had put some sort of spell on the clothes she had given me. I immediately went and got those clothes and threw them out. I felt a little crazy thinking this, but it didn't hurt to get rid of the clothes she had given me.

    I was trying to find answers to many things at once and was beating myself up for not 'getting it.' I'm intelligent. I was having a problem that I was not getting what I was supposed to, from what I was experiencing. My mind was racing all the time with constant thought. I was thinking so fast sometimes I would forget what my last thought was. Some of these thoughts were emotional, they seemed to disappear as quickly as they came to me. I was having flashes of memories and glimpses of patterns of behavior toward me throughout my lifetime. Sometimes when I was trying to recall what I was thinking I would smell the essential oil that Lyn had used during my healing session. I knew that as these things were happening to me, they were essentially rewriting me in a way. As if the garbage was being taken out and I was learning how to let go of it. So, I could see what happened and rewrite my patterns of behavior, feelings, beliefs and thoughts.

    I thought maybe I should rule out any medical issues. I was in a position with my medical insurance. I had to wait for three months before seeing my doctor. That three months was almost up. I called my insurance company to see if it was possible to get in sooner and they suggested that I go to either urgent care or the emergency room. I had gone to urgent care and was prescribed nine different medications for what the doctor thought were raging infections of the ear, nose and throat. I knew I didn't have any infections. I have had sinus infections and they are very painful - I didn't have any pain.

After a week, I still wasn't feeling any better, so I decided to go to the emergency room. The emergency room doctor diagnosed me with having allergies and I was prescribed antihistamines. It was ridiculous feeling so sick and the doctors couldn't find anything seriously wrong with me. A few weeks later, I had my doctor's appointment and did lab work. The lab work showed that my glucose, HDL and Chloride levels were just slightly higher than average. My DHEA sulfate was by far higher than the rest of the lab results. I researched what this was and how I could change this. I found something interesting in my research and it correlated higher DHEA sulfate levels with PTSD. I don't think that the medical field has done enough research on this subject.

I had been reading "Repressed Memories: A Journey to Recovery from Childhood Sexual Abuse" by Renee Frederickson. In the book she discusses PTSD and sexual abuse. I thought that it was possible for me to be suffering from PTSD all my life and not know it. And here I was finding a correlation between PTSD and this elevated DHEA sulfate. I was starting to believe that I suffered from PTSD and never knew it. I never felt any other way than what I felt, so how would I know that I could feel any different. Was it possible for me to have lived with PTSD all my life and not be aware of it? It was a possibility.

Master in the Making

"Repressed Memories: A Journey to Recovery from Sexual Abuse" helped me a lot. I knew I wasn't alone. I knew there were far worse cases than mine. The book covered some methods of how to retrieve the repressed memories. It made me question whether or not my mother may also have been sexually abused. The book talked about the different roles that family members play around sexual abuse victims.

My supernatural experiences got weird, and they were about to get weirder. I developed rashes, but they weren't itchy rashes. I had a set of rashes that emerged on my legs: Imagine if somebody had poured boiling hot water on your legs and what the redness would like from the burn without any blisters. That's what this rash looked like. It was the oddest thing. I paid attention to how I was sitting to see if they would go away with a different position. The rash remained for over an hour.

I also experienced leg shaking when sitting. It was more of a rumbling, like a tremor. I had only previously experienced this when I was sitting in my backyard, lost in thought. This time I couldn't control the shaking and it would come in little spurts. I had never experienced anything like it. I knew I probably wasn't sick with anything that would cause it. I knew it was related to whatever I was going through spiritually.

In my searches on the internet of all the things that were happening to me. I was learning why I was going through all this weird shit. I read multiple websites on the same subjects. Each subject would lead me to another subject. I wanted to have a clear basic understanding. Trust me, I don't believe everything on the internet. It was important for me to have more than a dozen sources with the same information. I wanted to be sure that if I was self-diagnosing, that I was diagnosing myself properly. I surmised that I was going through a Spiritual Awakening and I was also dealing with the Dark Night of the Soul. Spiritual Awakening and Dark Night of the Soul seemed to fit the rashes, legs shaking, insomnia, racing thoughts, night sweats, etc. and not having anything medically wrong with me.

One afternoon as I was sitting at my desk chair in my living room shredding paper, I experienced the taste of cilantro in my mouth. I hadn't eaten any cilantro, nor did I have any in or around my home. The taste of cilantro became stronger and stronger, it was as if I was *actually eating* it. In my mind I heard my mother say, "Oh this is so good, oh my god this is so good." My first impulse was to call my mother and ask if she was eating cilantro. I didn't call her. I waited a couple of days and asked her about this experience of eating cilantro and it being good. She confirmed that she in fact had been eating cilantro and eats it on a regular basis.

This was an odd experience that I don't recall ever having had before. It didn't freak me out. I was in awe and taken aback. It was making me more aware that maybe I was manifesting some spiritual perceptions; this one being Clairgustance, meaning 'clear tasting.'

I thought maybe I should pay more attention to my intuition and be more aware of my senses. I was sensing that I was supposed to become a spiritual healer. I had no idea what was in store for me and what I was put here to do.

A day or two after tasting cilantro, I woke up at three once again. That morning I was smelling some stinky perfume. You know the kind that maybe 'Patty the daytime hooker' would wear? The kind of perfume that gives you a headache and makes you gag. The smell seemed to be coming from the backyard and I thought; well, my bartender neighbor was wearing a new perfume, or she had a friend over. I hadn't smelt it before and never smelled anything but weed from my bartender neighbor's yard. I went back inside the house, but I could still smell it. I went back outside, and the scent was getting stronger and stronger. It was happening again, but this time I couldn't pin it on a person. All I was picking up with my intuition was that this person lived northeast from me. My logical brain went through my friends list of whom might wear perfume like that. I contacted one of my friends and she said she had bought some new perfume, but it wasn't making her sick. I was telling my friend Cyndee about these things that were happening to me. She told me that on the day I had smelt the perfume, one of her co-workers had worn some smelly perfume that made her sick. Cyndee's workplace had a 'no fragrance' policy; that day it was broken. Funny thing is, Cyndee did live northeast of me. What was coming next? I had no idea. All I could say to myself was: *"Buckle up bitch and brace yourself!"*

    I was searching for answers. I didn't know what to read. I didn't know who to go to for help. I tried listening and dancing to music. I started to go back to the things from my late teens and early twenties that made me feel happy, strong and free. I had gone to many concerts in Berkeley and San Francisco. One of the bands I had seen was Operation Ivy at 924 Gilman Street. I would find different music on YouTube and Spotify to listen to. I stumbled upon Tim

Master in the Making

Armstrong's music. First, I listened to "Tim Timebomb and friends," then "A Poet's Life" and then finally a Transplants song "DJ, DJ." The lyrics of "DJ, DJ" spoke to me. It was my medicine. It was my power. I adopted "DJ, DJ" as my theme song. Later I adopted "Into Action" as my theme song and even have it as my ringtone to this very day.

Music and dancing have always played a big part of my life. My dad played the drums and there were many weekend mornings that I would be awakened by the sound of drums and music. I remember doing 'the bump' with my brother Greg when "The Hustle" would be played. I can't remember if my dad had played for money before I was ten, but I know that he had played at a few bars when we had moved back to Modesto. My dad learned to play the drums by ear. He also played the trumpet and the piano by ear. My mother had taken piano lessons when she was a child. My father bought my mom a piano when I was five years old. We had a room designated as 'the music room' at our house in Fair Oaks. I never played any instruments as a child but have always wanted to learn how to play the drums.

I have always had an appreciation for music. I would listen to Casey Kassem's top forty countdown on the radio every Saturday. I think I attended every single high school dance. But it wasn't until my late teens that music really became influential in my life. I listened to a lot of different music. You can keep classical or country, it's not my genre. Anybody who listens to music will have a music soundtrack to their lives and what was happening in their lives at the time that a song was popular or playing. The music we hear stays with us and reminds us of those times. I had been to some bigger concerts by the time I was eighteen, but it was

Master in the Making

the smaller venues that intrigued me; that's where a nobody band could be the next big thing or have the next big sound in music. 924 Gilman street is an all ages club in Berkeley. It was one of those smaller venues. It still exists today. Graffiti covers absolutely everything, including the toilet seats. It was just so 'punk rock.' It was cool. I felt free at this time, because I was about a hundred miles away from home and experiencing life. I was fortunate enough to get to see Operation Ivy play twice at Gilman street, shortly before they disbanded. Tim Armstrong was a singer and guitarist in Operation Ivy. Later he and former bandmate Matt Freeman formed the band Rancid, among his other music projects. It's probably coming off as though I have a crush on Tim. That's not the case. I have a respect for him as a storyteller. He's a songwriter, but it's through his lyrics that his story is revealed. Tim tells it like it is. I connect with the music, lyrics and stories. That's it, it's as simple as that.

Operation Ivy has been credited as being one of most influential bands that had incorporated punk rock with ska and in turn creating a unique style of music. Operation Ivy's music has influenced many different bands and many bands have done covers of their songs. Green Day is one of those bands. Green Day gives credit to Operation Ivy for the beginning of their music career. Operation Ivy helped Green Day get a gig at 924 Gilman street. As far as I know to this day, Green Day will pull audience members onto the stage to play Operation Ivy's song "Knowledge."

I wasn't going to tell this story but it's a story I tell repeatedly; maybe this will be the last time I tell it. In 1989 I had taken a friend of mine to a Social Distortion concert at the Fillmore. The opening band was playing, and we didn't

Master in the Making

have any interest in seeing them. We were outside a couple of blocks away smoking. Three guys approached us with this plastic milk crate full of 45's that they were selling. I can't remember how much they were selling them for, but we didn't buy one. I regret not buying one. They seemed very full of themselves proclaiming that they were going to be the next big thing. We had gone back and forth with them about how cool Operation Ivy was and that they probably hadn't seen them. Joke was on us, they knew them personally. Well, those three guys turned out to be Green Day. It's kind of a cool story. Like how Parker was best friends with Kurt Hammond of Metallica and went to school with Les Claypool.

8
You Don't Know How It Feels

    In search for answers, I went to a used bookstore. I think I was looking for metaphysical or spiritual books, but when I got there, I saw Friedrich Nietzsche's "Beyond Good and Evil." Something told me to buy it. I was feeling very lost. I felt very disconnected in the sense that I really didn't have anybody to talk with about what I was going through. I finally felt comfortable with being alone and by myself. It had taken months to feel content to be myself and not need anybody else around. I had been surrounded by people in my home for over twenty years. I have had the attention span of a gnat since I left my husband, but now I was able to focus my attention for longer than an hour. I was able to sit and focus.

    Earlier in my life I had taken a philosophy class and read Nietzsche. I had even adopted Nietzsche's quote, "that which does not kill us, makes us stronger" as my motto that I used to live my life by. As I grew older, I felt like it was a challenge from me to the universe, so I stopped using it as my motto. I did enjoy Plato's "Republic" and the deep thinking it provoked in me. I don't recall which Nietzsche book I had read in that philosophy class. I knew I had to read the book that I just bought; "Beyond Good and Evil." I think the most important thing I had gained from reading that book at this time in my life was validation. I was enjoying Nietzsche's tongue-in-cheek style. I was feeling like he was a punk rocker because he was so antagonistic.

Nietzsche made arguments about 'righteousness' and what that looked like in society. Was it necessary to go to church? Was the bible really given in the context that it was originally meant to be? Was the bible and the church used to control man and society? By going to church and subscribing to the beliefs and practices, was it going to get one into heaven? Could one buy their way into heaven with money or power? Nietzsche's book also validated my thoughts, feelings and beliefs toward God and religion; I experienced guilt at times for not belonging to a church. I didn't want to go to church, because in my opinion that's where condemnation is bred; guilt, shame, judgement, etc. That's where all the bible thumping and soapbox propaganda happens. I never wanted to be a part of it. Who am I to judge another? It's not my place to judge another, nor is it anybody else's place to judge me and my relationship with God. I didn't need that in my life, nor did I want it. Besides that, my God, the God I know, is all forgiving. The God I know, knows my heart and mind. He loves me just as I am and knows I work every day to be the best person I can be.

I was feeling disconnected from God. I thought about what my brother had said about having spirit guides and that they pushed us and that is probably why I was being woken up in the middle of the night. They were pushing me to think about things and to find solutions. These lessons I needed to learn. I had a different belief than my brother on spirit guides. I believed that they were there to help us and guide us. I mentally and verbally spoke out to my guides and angels. I asked them for a sign that I wasn't alone, and that I *wasn't* going crazy. I was afraid I was losing my mind. The fact that I had repressed memories and had been in denial for forty-four years concerned me very much. What else had I repressed? I was very, very tired and needed my sleep. I explained to my spirit guides and angels that I existed in time, that I operated and ran by a clock here on earth and that I needed to sleep at least a couple more hours a night. I made a deal with them that I would continue to work on what I needed to work on in exchange for sleep. I had to do this a few times and explain that I couldn't think clearly to work on my stuff without sleep. Yep, I sound totally fucking nuts!

Well, what do you know I was sleeping until four or five, instead of the dreadful three A.M. I was still very tired and felt like I needed to catch up on a lot of sleep. I started to feel something on my left arm. It felt as though somebody had their hand gently gripping my upper arm. No, I wasn't having signs of a heart attack or a stroke! I wasn't exactly sure who or what this was. I knew it was friendly and there to let me know that I wasn't alone in what I was going through. To this day, every now and then I feel this gentle grip. Now, I try to remember what I was thinking about when I feel this grip on my arm, so that I might be able to correlate it with something outside of not being alone or were they trying to tell me something else?

My parents weren't in the best health. My father had bladder cancer and had been in remission for a couple of years, but his doctor recently discovered another serious illness. My mother had been diagnosed with a serious illness as well. She said she wasn't in pain and that she feels fine. She opted to forgo any type of traditional western medicine. She said she was being treated by a chiropractor who practiced alternative and holistic medicine. The main source of her treatment was a grounding pad, a Rife machine and a change in diet. This Rife Machine was connected to a computer that had different programs for different ailments. It was interesting to me. The machine would emit sound, light and electrical frequencies that purportedly vibrate in the body so that healing would take place. I even tried it a few times. I'm not sure if it helped me. I tried a foot detox bath, but I wasn't sold on what it was supposed to do.

    My dad wasn't one to subscribe to the idea of holistic or alternative medicine and had been actively looking for a surgeon who was highly skilled for a medical procedure. I was willing to drive my dad to Sacramento, Davis or San Francisco if he needed somebody to and I had made it known that I would. I sensed that my brother Greg and my mother were trying to talk him out of having the procedure done. Last I heard about this, is that my dad didn't have the procedure and started using the Rife machine.

9

Photograph

The repressed memories weighed heavily on my mind. I was trying to meditate to retrieve the memories of what had happened to me. I was slowly remembering little bits and pieces of my trip to Canada. I remember my mother holding me and handing me to my Grandfather and that my Grandfather didn't seem like himself. At three years old I was picking up a sinister type vibe from him, possibly his energy. I was given to him so that he could put me down for a nap in one of his treatment rooms. He was a chiropractor and had the front ground level part of the house converted to a large office with smaller treatment rooms. I remembered being on the floor in that treatment room and the whole trauma of him not giving me my underwear. I remember the car ride to the lake. I was trying to be very careful not to make up things that really didn't happen.

I tried dream prompts, such as; "what happened next?" I was hoping my memory would come to me in a dream. I wasn't certain how many trips to Canada we had made before I was twelve or how many trips my Grandparents had made out to California. I wondered how many times I had been abused by him. I wondered what my trigger was that would result in this snippet of a memory to come to me. I had this flashback come to me for years. I had no idea what my triggers were.

Master in the Making

A friend of mine called me; he has been a confidant for the past few years, but I hadn't spoken to him in a couple of weeks. I was going to share with him all the things I was going through. I was going to tell him about the repressed memories of sexual abuse that I had just uncovered. He seemed like he needed to tell me something, so I waited to tell my story. I was not prepared to hear what he had to tell me. He told me that he had just recently uncovered his own repressed memories of being sexually abused by an uncle when he was just four or five years old. I was like WTF? I asked, *"Wait a minute you are going through this right now?"* He said he told his mother that he had been sexually abused as a child, over the past weekend. His mother didn't dispute it with him. He said he couldn't remember the sexual act, but he does remember waking up having a sore behind and feeling as though he had been violated. Interesting that he came to me to share this with me. He *too* had a repressed memory and he *also* denied that his memory was true. Unlike me, he didn't want to know exactly what had been done to him. I still wanted my memory. Not being able to access and recall a memory was very disturbing to me.

In the hope of retrieving my memories, I went back to Lyn for another chakra healing and balancing. This time my session was a little different. I had asked for my spirit guides, angels, archangels to accompany and protect me. I was still leery of the spiritual healing and more importantly the healers working on me since my experience with Reiki. Lyn worked on me for nearly an hour. I cried like the last time but this time, I was focusing more on the sensations I was having. The energy in my forehead was still whirling about like flubber. When Lyn was done working on me, she shared with me what she had written down during the session. There wasn't as much on this piece of paper compared with the first time I went to her. One of the main things that she had written down was something with my left eye and to have it checked out. She said that when she was working on me that she felt a very sharp pain in her left eye.

    I do recall her working on my head and having this sensation that this energy poked her. While this energy poked her, there was a part of me that was laughing inside. It was like my subconscious laughing or possibly something else. Consciously, I would not do such a thing. I had been suspecting that this swirling flubber was possibly my spiritual gifts wanting to manifest. I didn't want to hurt Lyn and I did not have control over poking her in the eye at all. I wasn't in control of this energy and I had no idea how to manage it. I sensed that my energy or spiritual gift was a mischievous jokester. Even if I didn't have my repressed memories, at least I had a new experience to share and I thought it was a funny one.

    I asked my mother if I could go through all the old family photos. I was trying to piece together anything as well as trying to jog my memory. My whole body was very tense while looking through the photos. My mother was sitting at the table with me and looking at the photos with me. I got the sense from her demeanor that she was afraid that I would find something out about her, like I was going to expose her somehow. I was able to piece together that there had been two different trips to Canada. One in 1973 and another in 1974, from there I was able to determine I was three years old and the abuse happened in 1973. I had looked at these photos repeatedly over the years.

Master in the Making

One of the photos was me when I was almost two. I was standing next to a stroller that my brother Steven, was in. I have had this scar on my left arm for years and I have always debated with my mother that this scar was from me scratching at a vaccination I had gotten. She insisted that the vaccination had been on my right arm. My mother tried to convince me that my memory was incorrect, every time it was brought up. In looking at that photo of me at the age of two, I pointed out to my mother that the cotton ball and tape on my left arm was from a vaccination I had gotten, and it is exactly where my scar is. In fact, my mother had a scar from a vaccination she had gotten as a child. Her scar and my scar are in the very same area and both on our left arms. I wondered why my mother would try to convince me that my memory wasn't true, especially over something so trivial. I understand you don't remember everything that happens to your children as you grow older, but this went further than that. I physically showed her our scars were in the same area in almost the same spot on our left arms.

I remember a lot of things from my childhood. I guess this was a process to show me that I did remember a lot of things. There was one time when there was a big fire in the court behind our house. I remember that there were a couple of fire trucks and I could see the roof in flames. I was little and had to stand on my bed to see out the window in the direction of the fire. I went to tell my mom. She didn't believe me and told me to go back to bed. Then my dad came into my room and looked. He went back to tell my mom that there *was* in fact a fire. I was two and scared. I don't remember either one of my parents hugging me or consoling me. I was just told to go back to bed. Whenever I have brought this up with my mother, she *does* remember the fire and her reasoning for not getting out of bed is because she was too tired.

I went home with the photos and would reread the book I had purchased about repressed memories. I was slowly getting more of my memories, but the one I wanted to know most about is what was done to me by my Grandfather. One of the memories is of me looking my mother straight in the eyes and telling her about my missing underwear. She had my brother, Greg in her arms and she blew me off. She told me to go cry somewhere else and literally turned her back on me. When I retrieved this memory, I think I was denying to myself about who my mother really was. I had denied to myself about who my mother was my entire life. It would take me a few more months to admit this to myself. To this day this is probably the worst part of having been sexually abused. It wasn't entirely what my Grandfather had done to me, it was what my mother had done to me afterwards.

I know I was only three at the time, but I knew in the core of my being, that my mother knew that something horrible had happened to me. I was hurting and hurting badly internally at that moment and needed my mommy. I needed her to hold me and love me. But I didn't get that. I felt completely abandoned by her. I think more than anything she couldn't process it and deal with what she suspected had happened. She made a conscious decision to ignore it, and to deny to herself that it happened. She wouldn't have to deal with it. She hadn't listened to me or believed me or took care of my needs.

Master in the Making

It concerns me in being a mother myself. I wonder if I had ever behaved this way with my own children. Did either one of my boys suffer something traumatic that I never picked up on? There's a part of me that truly believes I wasn't that kind of mother. I know that I could detect an ear infection in my eldest son just by looking at him. My first indication was just looking into his eyes, they would be glazed, his forehead would be warm. I would ask him how he was feeling and if his ears were hurting. I would make him a doctor's appointment and every time he would be diagnosed with an ear infection.

There were a couple more glimpses of memories. One memory was of being at my Aunt and Uncle's Cabin which was North of Toronto. I was outside, about three to five feet from the side of the cabin and my Grandfather was closer to the cabin. I felt panicked, I shook my index finger at him to let him know that he wasn't going to get me again and then I ran away; probably to find safety with my brothers and cousins. At the end of the trip to the cabin, we had gone to see another Aunt at her apartment in Toronto. We sat on her balcony which was either the second or third floor. We drank soda out of these short cans that at that age I don't remember ever seeing short cans and thought they were cool. I can see the inside of the apartment in my head and can recall the layout. I can remember sitting there thinking of telling my Aunt what my Grandfather had done to me. I was searching my three-year-old vocabulary for words to describe what he had done. I ran dialogue through my head as to how I would tell her in hopes that she would understand me and be the one last person, the one last adult I felt I could tell this awful event to. I do remember telling her and her reaction was not what I had hoped. I remember her telling my mom what I had told her, but I cannot remember what was said. I probably blocked that memory out of my mind too. I am sure that at three years old I was devastated. It was probably my last attempt at telling an adult before my mind had decided out of self-protection and survival to repress the memory.

After reuniting with my family after five years, I would go out to my parents' house every now and then. I was starting to notice that my mother would make some snide remarks to me. I really can't think of the actual words she said or what they were about, but those words hurt me. My immediate innate reaction was to ignore what she said. As I noticed this behavior in her and how I was responding to her, I started to pay closer attention to what was being said and how I was reacting to it. One evening, I had some time before my Bunco group was meeting, so I stopped by to say hi. We were out in the single detached garage where the tractor was stored. My mother and brother Greg were sitting next to each other and I declined to sit. I'm not sure how the conversation turned to sexual abuse, but Greg said, "We have all been sexually abused at one time or another." Greg said if you think about it, we all have been sexually abused whether in this lifetime or a past lifetime. My mother agreed with him. I was absolutely shocked at what was just said and I didn't completely absorb what they were doing at the time. It wasn't so much what they were saying to me. I felt it was more to the effect that they didn't want to address my feelings and how I felt about what happened to me. I felt that they were discounting what had happened to me. They were discounting my feelings and what I was going through. I looked at them both, and one thing I thought was that my mother always went along with whatever Greg said, believed what Greg said and praised Greg relentlessly. He was the favorite child. That's not just my opinion or my observation of the relationship between my mother and my brother. My husband had made that observation and had indicated that is what he thought. My half-sister, Tara recently told me that she had the same impression I think I have always known this, but never wanted to admit it to myself.

Regardless of Greg being the favored child. My mother and brother weren't being empathic, sympathetic or caring toward me about the abuse I had suffered. It was as if they just wanted to diminish my experiences. These were my family members who were behaving this way toward me. These were the people who were supposed to love, care for, support, protect and help me. I think that not having been in contact with my family for five years really helped me step back a little and evaluate what had probably been going on all my life.

One of the reasons I had stopped talking with my family was over me hounding my mother to get my brother Greg help. I hadn't seen who my brother Greg really was until I was trying to help him get joint custody of his daughter. In the child custody court order, it had required him to go to narcotics anonymous meetings. He still needed to attend the meetings. He didn't want to go alone, so I agreed to go with him. I was picking him up, attending the meetings and then dropping him off. In doing all of this with him, I was getting to know who my brother Greg was. He felt at ease talking to me and started telling me these things he was experiencing.

Master in the Making

He told me that he thought that groups of people were following him and tracking him. He thought that these groups of people communicated to each other with their car headlights during the day about his whereabouts. He said that they would sneak into his house and move or take things. He said that they would make noises to get his attention. He thought everybody was out to get him. He also thought that these people could read his mind. I also saw that my brother had taped foil on a small folding table, the back of his door and part of a wall behind a dresser in his room. I was having a hard time seeing what my brother was going through. I was seeing that it was a struggle for him with all these things going through his head. I imagined myself living like he was, and it was just horrible to think about the torment he was going through.

Greg was living with my parents at this time, and one weekend my parents had gone out of town. I was going to drop by and check on Greg while they were out of town. For some reason I didn't make it there. I called him instead and he told me that people were knocking on the outside of the house and that something was missing on his dresser. He told me that he had gotten our dad's rifle out, loaded it and was ready to use it. This is where I drew the line with all this nonsense. If I had gone there to visit my brother, I could have been shot. I could have been killed by my own brother. I feared for my parent's safety as well. What if Greg hurt one or both my parents? When my parents got back from their trip, I called my mother and brought this up with her.

I told her about the gun and her response and resolution to the problem was to have the gun in one room and the bullets in another. WTF? Right? I was angry with her over this. This wasn't going to solve the problem. I looked for outside resources to possibly help my brother. At this point, I was on my mother's back to get Greg help. I was giving her resources I had found that might help. My mother didn't want to admit to me that something was wrong. At the same time she was saying that she didn't want to see him on medication or in an institution, she was also denying that there was anything wrong with him at all. In fact, she said he was just fine and that there wasn't anything wrong with him. I had badgered her so much about getting help for Greg that she told me I was stressing her out and that I was going to cause her to have a heart attack. That's when I decided to back off. This is what caused my mother to stop speaking to me. I'm assuming she didn't want to deal with the issue. It was pointless to talk about it anymore to anyone.

After that brief visit before bunco to my parents, I decided to keep my distance from them. I was keeping busy reading books, searching the internet, watching the television and working. I had reunited with Landon, a good friend of my other brother. I was helping Landon and his mom to find a home to purchase. We reminisced about the other kids in the 'hood. Landon had lived two doors down from my best friend, Shelly. He asked if I still talked to her. I was friends with her on Facebook, but we hadn't spoken in years. He asked me to tell her hello for him through messenger. I did. Shelly could not remember Landon. That was incredible to me to hear, because these two had been neighbors for at least ten years. Shelly and I began texting and talking more than we had in years.

I knew that there was a reason that I had been reconnected with Shelly. I was trying to figure it out. Shelly was living in Texas and I had an intuitive impression that I was either going to visit her in Texas or that I was going to be moving her back to California. I knew Shelly was depressed and needed to be back in California around her family again. She had moved to Texas just prior to her younger sister passing away from a battle with breast cancer. By the end of July, Shelly and I had plotted a plan to move her back to California. At the end of August, I was to fly to Texas then we would drive the already packed up U-Haul back to California. We made plans to stop and see some of those cheesy roadside attractions and the Grand Canyon. I was so excited to be taking a trip. I was nervous and had some fears about traveling by myself. It had been over twenty years since I had taken a trip alone.

    I told Greg and my mother that I was going to go get Shelly. Greg suggested that I visit the vortexes in Taos, New Mexico. I had no idea what a vortex was and why he was making a big deal about it. Yep, you guessed more google searches and research ensued! I wasn't sold, and I'm still not sold on vortexes. I'm sure that my view on these things will change in the future. I had to go see what the big deal was about in Taos, New Mexico. I was looking to do some more energy healing while I was there. I was curious if anybody else could help me get those memories I so desperately wanted. I consulted Shelly to see if it would be okay if we made a long drive off our path to Taos. It was cool with her, so I began a search to find a healer who I might want to go see. I found one, but they were all booked up because of the Labor Day weekend. I had to go with my second choice. Knowing that it was going to be holiday weekend and Taos was going to be filled with tourists, I had to get an appointment immediately.

Around this time, I was starting to do things for myself in a way that nobody else had, nor had I in my entire life. All my life I had gone without or had to wait for things I wanted or needed. Growing up there were times when I wanted something like new shoes, new clothes, etc. It seemed like I was always the one who got taken care of last as a child. And while married, my husband and the kids always came first. I would sacrifice and go without. I decided that I wasn't going to do that any longer. I booked myself my first massage. When I was married, I had wanted to become a massage therapist, but my husband argued back and forth with me about massage parlors and masseuses being sleazy, dirty and distasteful. Especially not a place for his wife to be associated with.

I was tired and worn out by. My body hurt as well. I had a Swedish deep tissue massage. I ended up adding a dry brush massage as well. I had read about dry brush massages and how they are used to help the lymphatic system drain. I was very much enjoying the massage. I heard some women in the hallway talking while I was on the table. I knew somebody was walking down the hallway, but I didn't know who. I felt my gut respond to this person. I knew it was Lyn. I hold a very high regard for her as a healer. I can only hope to be as good as her. I value her methods and hope to be able to implement them in my own healing practices.

About half way through, the therapist started to massage my left hand. It stirred something inside me to think of Parker and I burst into tears. I assumed that the touch triggered such an emotion, because the last person to touch my hand that way was Parker. Later I learned that the left hand is associated with the heart and that my heart was still breaking for Parker. Then she was gently working on my head and had my head held in a comfortable position for a long time. I find it is very hard for me to relax, even at home. I thought I wouldn't be able relax as much as I did during that massage. The position she had my head held in, was very relaxing. For a moment, I felt euphoric. I was happy at that moment and let out a giggle, I had no control over it. I had no idea why I had giggled, it just came out. Then I felt as though I was going to drift off to sleep. I think I had fallen asleep, because I heard myself snore and woke up.

When I flew into Fort Worth, I was supposed to have been picked up by Shelly's boyfriend. I think I was waiting for over three hours. I was pretty upset because I wanted to get on the road and go sightseeing. After waiting three hours at the airport, he finally showed up. Shelly hadn't gotten the U-Haul yet, so things weren't packed in the truck ready to go. In fact, her boyfriend and I had to drive from one U-Haul place to another. It was insane. On top of that her boyfriend had to get gas in his truck. There had recently been a hurricane and massive flooding in the southern parts of Texas, which caused a gas shortage in the state. There were lines of cars out of and around every gas station. It looked like the seventies gas shortage I remembered as a kid.

Six hours after my flight landed, I finally got to see my friend, Shelly and meet her two boys. I knew the living conditions I was going to see when I got there. Shelly had very vaguely described how she was living. I knew it was going to be much worse than she had let on. It was a little bit worse than I had imagined. I was glad I was helping my friend out of this situation. I was still upset by all the delays, but seeing what I saw, made me feel a little bit better as I knew I was doing something good. I had a feeling that I was meant to do this and that somehow, I would gain something from the experience or that maybe I needed to have Shelly in my life again for some reason. By nine in the evening, the U-Haul was packed, and we all were tired and hungry.

We were still in Texas and hungry, Shelly insisted that we have Whataburger. I hate it when people hype things up, so I didn't set my expectations too high on this Whataburger. It exceeded my expectations. It was rather tasty. Shelly had informed me of the Texas culture and how it contrasted to what we were used to in California. It was how she had described it. "Yes, ma'am. No, ma'am. Yes, sir. No, sir." Texans are very friendly and hospitable. We ended up staying the night in a hotel not far from the Whataburger. We didn't get to the border of Texas and New Mexico like we had planned to do. We made up for it the next day and drove and drove and drove. It was hot out and the U-Haul didn't have a bench seat, so the four of us were crammed into this two-seater U-Haul. We also had Brodie, Shelly's shiatzu. We cracked jokes about our exes, so happens Shelly's ex was from Texas. Isn't there a song about exes from Texas? I decided that Shelly's ex-boyfriend's name didn't fit him. I renamed him Cletus. If you saw this guy, you would agree it was more fitting for him than his own name. Just imagine a good 'ole boy named with a name like Fabio, Cletus fit better.

At that point, I won the trust of Shelly's teenage son, Rick. Rick had trust issues with Shelly's other friends and some family members. Rick picked up that he could trust me, and he warmed up to me almost off the bat. Shelly had even commented on how he had warmed up to me so easily. This kid is very special to me, he is my Ninja. Ron, Shelly's youngest son is very special to me too. As the months passed with Rick in my house, I felt blessed to have had spent time with him. He was the typical teenager who constantly ate and played video games. He reminded me of my own two sons and how sweet and kind my own kids were. We would converse about television shows.

    One night while we were both in the kitchen he said, "Hey my Ninja, you want to watch The Walking Dead with me?" I was so touched by this and I am to this day. I am crying about this as I write. I felt such joy about him asking me to share time with him. I was tired that night and was headed to bed. I declined his offer but expressed to him how much he touched my heart. See, my boys and I would watch The Walking Dead together and they too would ask me if I wanted to watch it with them. I kind of regret turning him down now, because I missed an opportunity to spend some time with this kid.

    These people have been through such turmoil in their lives. When Shelly and I were childhood friends, I knew things weren't right at home. I knew that there were things that Shelly had endured and never told me about, nor had I told her what I had endured as a child. Shelly had shared with me that she had been repeatedly sexually abused and that nobody had listened to, protected or helped her. She said she had always wanted to tell me what was going on at home when we were younger, but she was scared for some reason. She knew she could trust me then as she did now. She also confessed that one of the major struggles as a child for her was hunger. She told me that she would have to go into the nearby grocery store to steal food for her and her sister to eat.

I had to confess to her that the picture of this happy family she thought I had as a child was a complete lie. My dad was an alcoholic and that there was a lot of yelling and drama in my household. Shelly and I couldn't remember how we spent all our time together, but we did know it involved 'Light Brights,' a couple of 45's Rick James "She's a Super Freak," Joan Jett's "I Love Rock 'n Roll" and a Go Go's cassette tape. We figured that we were always trying to escape our own home lives, so we took solace in each other's company. We would spend our summer days at her house either until the pool opened at the high school, or until her mom got home. We split once her mom got home. If we were at my house playing, she knew when my dad got home it was time for us to go.

My parents didn't have a very high regard for Shelly. When we were young teens, we started smoking cigarettes. To this day both my parents blame Shelly as the reason why I began smoking. By the way, both my parents are smokers and cigarettes were readily available to me at home when I started smoking. Well, I gave Shelly an addiction as well. When she came to live with me, I introduced her to 'Stella Rosa' wines. I didn't make her an alcoholic, but she has since then had an appreciation for Stella Rosa wine.

We arrived late in Taos, with my healing and reading scheduled for the next day. I was hoping to find the answers to what happened with the Reiki and my memories. Shelly dropped me off in the U-Haul at this little shop where my appointment was. I went inside and checked in for my appointment. As usual, I was early. I was nervous. I tried to kill time by going a couple of shops down for a bottle of water and just sit and collect my thoughts. I went inside and looked around at the crystals, which didn't appeal to me. I wasn't interested in crystals at all. I had one purple quartz crystal necklace way back when I had dated a Deadhead. There were chakra wall hangings all around me. They had books and artwork as well. I didn't identify with all the crystals. I used the restroom and when I came out this woman was coming in with a 'to go' coffee cup. It was obvious she worked there. She asked me if we knew each other. I didn't know her. I had never been to Taos. I told her I didn't think we knew each other and that I was there to a have a reading and healing. She introduced herself as Marsha. I was her next client and she said she would be right with me.

After a few minutes, Marsha came out of the room she had gone into and led me through the shop to a door and then into a hallway. The right side of the hallway was lined with floor length windows and the left side was rice paper screens like you would see in a Japanese restaurant. There were a set of screens that opened to a good size room. In this room I saw crystals on a bookshelf, a massage table, and a table of singing bowls and hand drums. The singing bowls reminded me of when I had first met Lyn for my chakra healing and balancing. Lyn had told me about when she had gone for a healing and the woman used singing bowls. Lyn had said she didn't get anything out of it, except for a headache from all the damn singing bowls.

I laid down on the table and closed my eyes. I was a little disappointed that we had started with the chakra healing and balancing. I was really looking forward to the intuitive reading. Marsha asked if it was okay to use essential oils on me and I agreed that it was okay. This is what Lyn had done in our session, so it wasn't anything new to me. Marsha proceeded to tell me about how her Master had blended this oil just for her. In my head, I was thinking, okay big deal blending oils can't be that difficult. Marsha took different crystals and placed them on me and around me like Lyn had also done. She placed two small ones on my forehead, one in my left hand, a heavy one on my stomach and a few others here and there. This time I didn't have on any headphones and Marsha began to speak. What she was saying was coming out like a singing chant. "What they did was wrong! What they did was wrong! What they did was wrong!" Oh yeah, I knew that was spirit talking to me and saying what Delvin and Trisha had done was wrong. "Poor baby, oh poor baby." I didn't connect with that. "I need love, I need love!" She said that repeatedly as well. I wasn't really connecting to the meaning of that one either. Yeah, I longed to be in a romantic relationship again and I was still recovering from my breakup with Parker. I wanted and needed love.

  Marsha had played the singing bowls and at least three different drums. I had the same reaction to this healing. More crying. I wasn't connecting to why I was crying. Marsha removed all the crystals from me and around me. When I got up from the table, I was a bit dazed. Marsha was at the door waiting from me. She handed me two of the crystals she had used on my forehead. Both crystals were pyramid shape and the bases would fit on the head of a nickel. One was clear and the other looked like a world globe had been compressed into this little pyramid. She said that my spirit guide told her spirit guide to give me the two crystals, because I needed them. She said that they contained the record of what happened there that day. So, here I was, with two crystals and another new story.

Marsha led me out of the room and down the hallway to another room. She took a seat on the floor behind a low rectangular table. I sat down across from her. I saw tarot cards on the table and wondered if that was included in my intuitive reading. I felt that one of the questions I was there to get answered about Devlin and Trisha was already answered in the other room. I still didn't know what they had done, but at this point I was there to get my memories. I asked what had happened when I was sexually abused. She did not address my question the way I had wanted. Marsha said that I was very abused as a child. The only reference to abuse that I knew of was the sexual abuse and the enduring drama between my mother and father. Many nights I would fall asleep listening to yelling and screaming between the two. To me it was my normal. I knew nothing else growing up.

I felt that I wasn't really getting what I wanted out of the session. Toward the end of it, Marsha got excited and wanted me to meet her partner Kathryn, with whom she ran the shop with. To me it was a bit odd to have someone want to introduce me to a co-owner. Marsha was wanting me to talk to Kathryn about a detox counseling program she does. Marsha texted Kathryn to see if she was nearby. Marsha didn't get a response and as we were coming out of the room Kathryn was in the hallway. We all three went back into the room and sat down around the low table again. Marsha said something to me that made me leery. She said to me: "You have been working with somebody else and you really don't know if you want to work with them anymore. You should work with us. You really need to hear what Kathryn does. She's amazing." So, to be polite I sat and listened to what this whole thing was about. I was very skeptical and now I had my defenses up, especially because of what I had endured with the Reiki. I was feeling lured like a jackass with a carrot dangling in front of its face.

The detox consists of twenty-eight days of a very strict vegan diet and during that time I would meet daily for an hour with either Marsha or Kathryn. Kathryn looked at me and I knew that she was intuitively reading me. She said you have been having some eye problems and something going on with your liver, but you haven't been diagnosed with anything. She was correct with all of it. Lyn had told me to have my eyes checked out, she had also suggested that I take some Milk Thistle and drink grapefruit juice for liver health. My question was that if I did this detox would it help prevent me going on any medications in the future. They said that this would help. I didn't want to end up on any kind of medication, I didn't want to have to take a pill every day. This program came with a hefty price tag. They said that they could work out a payment plan with me for the program. I would be able to take all the supplies home with me that day, rather than having them shipped to me.

Even though something wasn't sitting right with me with these women and the situation, I decided to go ahead and try the program. I was still looking for answers and my memories. I made a good faith payment and waited for a box of supplies to be put together for me to leave with. Marsha carried the box out to the U-Haul and went back to her shop. I wasn't exactly sure where Shelly and the kids were. I looked in the cab of the truck and there they were waiting for me. I was a little emotional and wanted to tell her all about my experiences that I had just had. Shelly told me that something had come over her while she was walking around. She said that suddenly, she had been overcome with emotions and started crying. It was something that Shelly had never experienced before in her life. Between the two of us being in the emotional states we were in and the heat of the desert, we decided to forgo the hike to the vortexes and head to the hotel. We weren't in a big hurry to get back to California. All the emotional upheaval left us exhausted. We stayed another night in Taos.

    We made it back to California, skipping all the sightseeing we had planned, with the last leg of the trip being a long fifteen-hour drive. Chaos seemed to have been unleashed from the depths of 'god knows where.' Shelly had managed to misplace the last few hundred dollars she had to her name, as well as the padlock key for the U-Haul. The first hour or so upon arriving home was spent retracing our steps at the stops we had made. What made it more confusing was that there had been a power outage in an area we had tried to stop for gas; we had taken several exits and couldn't remember which exit we had taken and exactly where we had stopped and got gas.

    My mother had called me, and I was updating her on my adventures. Out of the blue she began talking shit about Shelly and was making it very clear that she didn't care for Shelly. She was telling me how to approach having Shelly in my home. She warned me of the consequences of doing what

I was doing. She was crossing a line with me; I became unglued, I was angry. I told her it wasn't up to her what I did, or how I did it. If there were repercussions from my generosity in the end then that would be on me and I would have to deal with it, not her. I questioned if she did not trust me or my judgement. I was an adult and she was telling me how to live my life.

I had been a little hurt over the prior few weeks that my mother hadn't come to my house to visit me. She had never seen my house. I had asked repeatedly but wasn't forceful in my requests. I asked her why she hadn't come to my house. She said she was in pain. That was the first that I had heard she was in any kind of pain. She had only said that she had pains that came with getting older. I took it as an excuse, because I felt that if it were my brother Greg asking her to come visit she would have. I even expressed this to her. Her response said it all: "You know Julie, we have different relationships with each one of our children." Internally, I thought *yes, I have my own children and I do have different relationships with them, but I certainly do not treat them different according to my relationship with them.* That's when I told her that I felt that "they" (meaning my mom and dad) never *really* loved me, and felt they never had. The conversation ended.

10

Trust

I was eager to begin the detox program, but I had more questions. I was feeling reluctant to move forward with it, because of the vibes I was getting. The 'carrot dangling in front of my face' feeling and what Marsha had said about me not feeling comfortable with the spiritual healer that I had been working with. I was questioning what was going to happen during these sessions. I wore them both out. I think they wanted to 'throw in the towel' before we had even started. I wanted help, but I wanted help. I felt Marsha was superficial and insincere. All of this made me leery and on guard. Marsha had spoken very highly of her master and she raved about him. She alluded to the idea that she could be my master. I really did not know what that meant at the time. I had done a little more research on the shop's website about who these two women were. They both had many spiritual gifts as well as had successful careers prior to becoming healers.

Another reason I felt reluctant about moving forward with the program was that Marsha had made a comment in my intuitive reading that she wasn't going to answer my questions about my abuse, because I was too sensitive. Marsha had compared her own story of abuse with mine. The only thing that our experiences had in common was that we were both violated sexually and had little memory of it. She had time to deal with not having the memory of her trauma. I had only recently realized what had happened to me and was still processing it. I was still processing the fact that I had repressed memories and that I couldn't completely recall everything that had happened. She never divulged if she had support from her family or if she ever told her family. I was three and I tried to tell my family, but nobody listened to me. I needed and wanted compassion and support.

    Out of the blue my sister, Tara called me to wish me a happy birthday. We hadn't spoken in a long while, I want to say many years. We had sent Facebook messages back and forth, but they were rare. It was nice to hear from her. Her birthday is three days after mine and she's two years older than me. I knew intuitively at the age of two that I had a sister, but I think as I got older, I ignored that I knew this. I didn't meet my sister until I was twenty-one when she had come to visit me in Tahoe. I had always wanted to embrace her as my sister. I never felt that I could wholeheartedly embrace her for some reason. I think I felt as though it was a betrayal to mother for some reason. I don't even know why I felt that way. I hadn't seen her in twenty-three years. The last time I had seen her was when she had come to stay for about a week when Alex was six weeks old. She was on her way to Guatemala to learn Spanish.

    I told Tara about becoming a spiritual healer and her response was how wonderful that I will be a healer like our Mom's dad: He was also a healer. He was a Chiropractor. Hearing that made me a little sick to my stomach. I then told her about what I had just discovered about my repressed memories and being sexually abused by him. I knew she had been a nurse at A Woman's Health Center for years and was trained in being compassionate in these situations, but the sincerity and compassion she showed me and how she apologized to me for what had happened to me was the only time I have ever felt that someone truly heard my story and cared about me. Her compassion was sincere and genuine. My boys did take me out to eat and gave me gifts and cards. Shelly and her boys made a Happy Birthday banner and card for me. My family didn't call me or send me a card to wish me a happy birthday on my birthday.

    A few days later my mother called to wish me a happy birthday. I was still angry from our previous conversation and the fact that she hadn't called me on my birthday. It made me feel very unloved by my mother. Somehow during our conversation, we ended up talking about my sexual abuse. She proclaimed that "she didn't believe me" and that "she wanted proof of the abuse." I wasn't one to make up stories or create drama for attention. I was not that kind of person for her to treat me that way. I was reeling with hurt. I was in tears. To me that was abuse on top of more abuse. I hung up the phone and that was the last conversation I ever had with her. How was my mother ever going to believe me? How was I supposed to give her proof of something that happened to me when I was three? How do you give proof of that happening anyhow? How could I ever talk to her or see her again? Why would I want to? There was still a part of me that didn't want to cut ties with her. I still wanted to love my mother. I didn't want to have to cut ties with my family again. I had just reconnected with my family after five years and here I was losing them again.

Master in the Making

During the days following, I remember speaking on the phone with Kathryn and somehow, I was convinced to move forward with the program. I had begun the actual detox a day or two prior to the first counseling session. I honestly had no idea what was going to unfold, or how I would benefit from the whole thing. The first few days I worked with Kathryn we used FaceTime for the counseling sessions. Nearly every day that I met with these women they would begin the session by looking at my face and taking a good look at me. Kathryn always took a closer look and it was more of a physical examination. It was as though she could see underneath my skin and into my brain. I would physically feel like she was poking around in my head. It was the oddest sensation and I had mixed feelings about her doing that.

When working with Kathryn, we had written down every physical illness I ever had. Then we looked at my emotional strengths and weaknesses. (I call this diagnosing metaphysical or spiritual illnesses. She called it something else.) I was familiar with spiritual illnesses from my internet research. Any physical symptom, disease or illness a person has, can be traced to an emotional problem. Once you are aware of an underlying emotional problem you can explore what may have caused it. This helps reveal the negative patterns that we live and were created by the trauma of an experience. I knew I had self-esteem issues. I had a hard time letting go of things. I had fears, I had a lot of unresolved grief and I wasn't happy. We dug deeper. There were more things uncovered, or rather things that were narrowed in on. Some of the things we uncovered was guilt, shame, anger, a sense of abandonment, extreme self-criticism, anxiety, rejection, passivity, emotionally closed off, depression, worrying, self-doubt, insecurity, unable to relax and trust, unrealistic expectations of myself and others, fear of being disconnected from my family, feeling like I didn't belong, rage, blocked passion, emotional instability and indecisiveness. Yep, so the result was that I was pretty fucked up.

    I kept some notes in a journal about these sessions. After a few days, Kathryn seemed to be finished with the deeper investigation as we switched gears and just seemed to be having more laid-back conversations. I told her that my legs had started shaking again and that I had the pressure in my head. She said that the leg shaking was getting rid of body tension and the forehead tension was related to my power of creation and manifestation of thoughts. I was still focused on trying to retrieve my memories. I knew that Marsha was too meek and afraid that I was going to completely unravel from her telling me something ugly. I felt Kathryn had a better understanding of me. I felt I could ask her. I felt that she would be more straightforward with an answer. When I asked her, she said that the sexual abuse was a violent penetration. She had me tell my body, my intestines and anus sorry for what had happened. So now I knew that he had sodomized me. Kathryn went on to say that it was energy abuse and that this trauma was in the memory of the cells of my body.

    This trauma violated my boundaries and left that impression on my energy field. In that session we also talked about if I felt like a slave. I felt that I needed to sacrifice myself. I did feel like a slave. I had felt that all my life. I felt I sacrificed my needs and desires for the people around me.

Master in the Making

She asked about what I needed to feel safe and secure. I needed money to provide the basics and I also needed my car. She asked why I needed a car. I needed a car, because I knew I had to go places and do things in my future. I couldn't give specifics. I didn't know exactly why I needed my car. I knew it wasn't necessarily for real estate work. She got this look on her face when looking into her mind's eye, as if she was looking into the future and understood why, because she said, *"oh I see."*

11
Karma

I believe this is about the time that I really began to grasp the concept of energy. Energy is everything. Energy is thoughts, feelings, emotions, memories, situations, places, circumstances and intentions. It is contained in our bodies down to the cellular level and in our DNA. Energy is in absolutely everything around us including inanimate objects; living or nonliving. Energies can be passed from one person to another. It can be passed down from our ancestors. It can be brought with us from past lifetimes and taken with us to the next. It can be trapped, or it can move in time. Energy is flowing in, out and through us all the time. Energy is also expressed in vibration, sound, color, scent and light. Energy can be negative or positive.

To take this one step further, if we as humans can realize that we carry these negative energies and can learn to let go of these negative energies it opens a space for positive energy to flow through us and heal us down to the cellular DNA level. It can heal us on the emotional, mental, spiritual and physical level. By doing this we can rewrite the direction and contents of our own lives. We get to rid ourselves of negative patterns that have kept us from being happy and productive.

Marsha worked more on spiritual and mystical, rather than emotional; which is what Kathryn did. The first day that Marsha and I worked together we talked about karma. We talked about generational karma and individual karma. We all have probably heard the biblical reference that the sins of the father carry down from one generation to the next for seven generations. This is also family karma aka generational karma. We also carry our own individual karma, not just from this lifetime but from our prior lifetimes. Marsha proceeded to tell me that I had a lot of karmic work to do, and that I had karma on both sides of my family. On my mother's side it was "pretending that everything is just fine" and "delusional darkness." On my father's side it was "stubbornness" and "that we power through things to completion." I laughed when I heard the karma on my dad's side, because it was so fitting. I did identify with the "pretending everything's okay," because I saw in it my mother. The 'delusional darkness' I had to look up online and investigate. I did see it in my mother. I didn't want to admit to myself that I also suffered from the karma of "everything is just fine." I wanted to deny that I too suffered from "delusional darkness," but I have since started realizing that I too suffer from it. The definition of 'delusional darkness' is: An irrational belief held with conviction, even when exposed to forms of proof that would otherwise contradict the belief; trouble recognizing reality, a false belief, and jumping to conclusions. After reading the definition of "delusional darkness," I knew then that my mother would never believe me even if I were able to give her proof of my abuse.

In that session, it was also revealed to me that I had a lot of psychic pain, from this lifetime as well as from my past lifetimes. I also had been a very powerful witch in a

Master in the Making

couple of my past lifetimes. I was able to manifest through spoken word. In one of those lifetimes I was a master in controlling my environment to the extent of being able to manipulate the elements. In one of those lifetimes I had misused my powers and it had a negative impact on five to six hundred souls. Hurting those souls was my individual karma. I had also been killed for my powers in a couple of my lifetimes. In this session Marsha told me that I still have those magical powers and that I am extremely powerful. She stated that I was so powerful that I had the equivalent of a PHD in magic. She said that my main spiritual gift in this lifetime is that of spoken manifestation. What does that even mean? Yeah, I get that what I say, and the intentions used behind what I say are powerful and can manifest things. Using a power like this must be done with care. What do you do with that kind of information? Obviously, I want to stay humble and not let it go straight to my head. I don't want to have any more repercussions of karma using my magic powers. Like I said earlier in this book; things get weirder and weirder.

    While in a session with Kathryn, she told me that I don't realize how much power I have. She said that when she first met me in the shop she knew, and that it was rare to meet somebody with such power. She said that I had so much power that I should have a robe and a staff and be looking out over a valley somewhere. Again, what do you do with that kind of information? Is this something they tell everybody? I really don't know what kind of powers I have. I do know that I will most definitely be careful using them. when I have them. Karma is a bitch! Who needs more bad karma?

Master in the Making

There was a lot said in that one session. The one thing that had been said, that weighed most heavily on me was that I was the seventh generation of this karma. It was my responsibility to 'clean the slate' so to speak. I was the one to end the generational karma from both family lines. *Why me? Why not somebody else?* Why was *I* chosen to end all this family karma? I still don't know to this day. I had no idea who or what situation created this karma I was to clean up. Doesn't it make you think about the karma you have created in this lifetime and what you may have passed onto your future generations? It made me think about that. It really made me think of the repercussions of my actions. I worried about any impact that I may have created upon my kids. Marsha gave me a karma prayer to say. I knew intuitively the prayer needed to be said aloud and with great intent. Over the course of the next few weeks I said the prayer repeatedly and addressed each family karma. I also focused on karma's that I may have created in this lifetime with people that I have known or know. It was very emotional work for me and I tried to make space and time to do it. At times I could sense that I hadn't done enough work on one or another of the karmas, so I would work on each until I felt I was relieved of it.

Kathryn and I went back to working on my deep emotional issues. I thought we had finished our investigation. I had a lot of built up frustration. I felt upset, angry and abandoned. I had a problem with speaking up for myself. My mother had told me during our brief union that I couldn't speak clearly and did not have a large vocabulary until I was four years old. I never recalled hearing this. I know it is something I would have remembered. I would have even been reminded of this when my eldest son Alex did not speak until he was four. I am pretty sure that it would have come up in conversation while going through it with Alex. Later, in this counseling, I learned that I was able to communicate with the limited vocabulary I did have when I was three. I was able to communicate what my Grandfather had done to me. The fact that nobody listened to my story caused me frustration that carried with me since then.

    Kathryn is very gifted spiritually and she was able to see that I was born into this world with anger and rage that had been passed onto me whilst my mother was pregnant with me. My mother had been very angry when I was born. I don't know why she was angry. Kathryn saw me as a baby in a walker. She saw that there was something wrong with me. She said that I was making jerking movements like epileptic seizures. She said I was crying and not like just crying but crying like a blood curdling cry that there is something wrong with me. She said there was something definitely medically wrong with me and nobody noticed. My parents had not noticed that I was having seizures. Nobody noticed that there was anything wrong with me. I asked where and what my parents were doing and if they could see what was going on. My parents were fighting with one another. I grew up with them fighting, arguing and yelling at one another. I didn't realize that it had been going on since I was a baby. It was constant drama between them. I was abandoned even though I was right before their eyes. I was basically neglected because they were too busy fighting with each other to pay attention to me. Maybe that's another reason I didn't speak clearly until I was four and had issues speaking up for myself as an adult. It is possible that I felt that speaking up would cause upset and conflict. I always avoided conflict in my life. It's possible that these things made me feel unloved, unwanted and that I didn't belong.

I wondered what could have caused me to have seizures. It could have been the stressful environment I was living in or it could have been something else. Either that night or one of the following nights after that session with Kathryn, I woke up around one in the morning. It had dawned on me that when Trisha did my Reiki, she had asked Devlin if I had issues with my ears. I told Devlin I had never had issues with my ears. Trisha had told Devlin that they came up as red and inflamed in the intuitive reading. At one in the morning I was searching the internet about ear infections causing seizures in babies. Of course, there it was on the internet on multiple websites. Severe ear infections in a child can indeed cause a child to have epileptic seizures. I never recalled having an ear infection in my life. My brother Steven had suffered a lot of painful ear infections as a child. I can't remember Greg having ear infections, but it is very possible. He had to have tubes put in his ears when he was around six years old.

Another interesting part of Kathryn's session with me was that I was surrounded by energy suckers and I had been all my life. You know that Devlin was an energy vampire which is another name for energy sucker. The people closest to me were energy suckers. Energy suckers drain our energy and when our energy is depleted it can lead to various symptoms. As a victim of an energy vampire you can feel dizzy, depressed, irritated, confused, angry, tired etc. You are probably wondering how to avoid an energy vampire. An energy vampire can take many forms. Energy vampires can be selfish and self-centered people who think the world revolves around them. They can be controlling, narcissistic, critical, angry, negative and blameful. They often lack empathy for others. In my case I was a people-pleaser. The people with whom I had close intimate relationships with were energy suckers. All my relationships were unbalanced. I gave more than I received. In other words, these people got more from me, than I got from the relationship, which in the end left me depleted of energy.

Reiki and Chakra healing and balancing are forms of energy healing. Once I started receiving these healings, everything began to go more haywire with the people around me. People in my life seemed to get pushier and more demanding. I even had a client at one time think that I was their own personal Realtor and that I should be available always just for them. Devlin's behavior was out of control. When you do energy healing your energy rises and is no longer compatible with those whom you have been surrounded by. So, one by one, the negative people and energy suckers around me left my life in one way or another. I reunited with my family and then they had to go again. I think I *had* to be reunited with them, so that I could put some of the pieces of my memory together. To see them for who they really are. This allowed me to not feel guilty for not speaking to them any longer. Regarding my husband and Parker. Parker came into my life for a reason and that reason was to be the pied piper, he had to be attractive enough to lure me out of my marriage, but also repulsive enough to get rid of him later. I honestly believe that God used Parker to help put me on the path I am on today.

Master in the Making

I didn't have a lot of time to digest and reflect on all the information that I was receiving day-to-day throughout the counseling sessions. It was a lot of information to take in, in only a matter of days.

12

This is your energy

Marsha had decided that I get my first lesson in playing with energy on one of the days I met with her. I was really, really, excited about this! I thought it was super cool to play with energy. She had me do this exercise where we clapped our hands together about a hundred times and then rubbed our palms together. You can find this exercise on the internet and I'm sure there are different methods out there. In fact, there are YouTube videos on it, too. Next, we took our hands with fingertips and thumbs tips facing one another, so that it looked as though we were holding an invisible ball. Slowly, we moved our hands inwards and outwards starting about an inch apart and then progressively moved outward until we felt a pulsing and pushing and releasing sensation between our fingers, thumbs and palms.

Before you decide to go and play with your energy (because I know some of you are going to try this), you need to protect yourself by only allowing pure and unconditional divine love to surround you. Then play all you want. I learned that you can also feel the energies of Archangels and Ascended Masters. I suggest you don't feel dark energies, as you can open a can of worms. I was able to feel Buddha's energy and it was very different than my own. I only had to do the above exercise about three times before I could just start moving my hands back and forth to feel my energy.

Master in the Making

Later, I would wake up and feel balls of energy in my hands like I had a weighted ball sitting on my palms.

In December 2017, I wasn't completely comfortable with playing with energy, so I had left it alone for a few months. One night I ended up hanging out with Parker and we had been partying. He had called me, whilst on his vacation. I wasn't interested in getting back together with him. I knew he hadn't and wasn't going to change. I hugged him from behind and told him that I still loved him very much. I walked away. He turned around and told me he loved me too. I did want validation that he still loved me. I wanted to hear it from his lips. He saw that there might be hope with having a relationship with me again. He started to talk about trying to make it work between us. I told him again that I couldn't because of me drinking too much alcohol. He told me to only have one or two and stop; but whenever I was with him, I didn't stop at one or two. I had to get a little mean with him. I told him that I was in a different place in my life and that I didn't want to be tied to anybody who had a commitment to younger children. I knew that was a blow to him and that I came off as uncaring. I really had to push him away. I kept telling him that I wanted to remain friends and that's why I was there. He asked if there had been anybody after him. I saw another opportunity to push him away further. I told him that I'd had sex with somebody and that I had a really good time with them. I don't know why I can't let go of people, especially him. There's still a part of me who wants to be with him; he's like a drug to me. I know he is no good for me, but I still wanted to be around him.

13
Good Vibrations

Parker had put on a Rush video and we were watching this long drum solo by Neil Peart. I closed my eyes and started playing with my energy, then I thought about feeling Neil Peart's energy. So, I started feeling his energy in my hands, but this time was a little different as I was seeing what the energy looked like in my head. Neil's energy felt a little like taffy; not as stiff as taffy but it felt like a controlled string on my fingertips and thumbs. His energy looked like different thicknesses of black lines that glowed this brilliant green color. I got the impression from Neil's energy that when he plays, he is very structured and very precise in his movements. I felt that he had been musically trained at some point and he was a perfectionist in his craft.

That night, I experimented with feeling my own energy. My energy is soft, white, billowy, cloudlike and has iridescent sparkles. I have asked other people who can feel energy to confirm this. I hadn't told these people what my energy looked like, nor felt like. Later, I tuned into Travis Barker's energy and it looked like and moved like a red [1]Hoberman sphere. I got the impression that Travis had some

---

[1] A **Hoberman sphere** is an isokinetic structure patented by Chuck Hoberman that resembles a geodesic dome, but is capable of folding down to a fraction of its normal size by the scissor-like action of its joints. Colorful plastic versions have become popular as children's toys: several toy sizes exist, with the original design capable of expanding from 15 centimetres (5.9 in) in diameter to 76 centimetres (30 in)

training but was mostly self-taught. His movements were controlled but that he was able to make more movements at one time; creative but with structure. Then there was John Bonham's energy and it was grey and black, but it had a thunderous heartbeat thump.

My lesson in playing with energy was an interesting one that ultimately led me to feel and see the energies of some powerful drummers. Why drummers? At that time, I had just begun taking drum lessons and was more interested in drummers' energies, rather than Archangels and Ascended Masters.

I was working with Kathryn again on my issues. I was discovering that it was hard for me to connect with my feelings, especially when it came to be dealing with my anger. I suppose deep down inside I was afraid of letting go, for fear I would lose control. I had the notion that admitting my anger existed was a bad thing. I was afraid of being bad. Kathryn told me that sometimes you must be bad for good reasons. I was always very passive, though I knew I needed to work on being assertive and dominant. It is a is a difficult role for me. I had been sensing for some time that this wasn't just from my present lifetime. I felt that some of my behavior was from a previous lifetime. I was requesting to have a soul retrieval done.

What is a soul retrieval? It is a ceremony, or ritual, that is performed to retrieve parts of the soul that may have gotten lost at any time during this lifetime or a past lifetime when something traumatic may have happened. The soul piece exists (never dies) in another dimension but must be asked to return to the soul. At my request for a soul retrieval, Kathryn dug a little deeper into my issues. She saw that in my last lifetime I had been a black female slave. I was a house slave who worked in the kitchen and inside the house. I was beheaded. Kathryn couldn't pick up why I had been beheaded, but I sensed that I had been killed for something that I didn't do. It had to do with something being stolen. Whatever happened in my prior lifetime it had something to do with me not being believed and it ultimately resulted in my beheading. I brought the energy of this traumatic event with me into this lifetime. A negative energy pattern that made me fear speaking up for myself. Kathryn said it was an unconscious karma.

Kathryn and I discussed me and my boundaries. Since I had all these relationships in the past that were unbalanced, I was to give myself permission to set and keep boundaries in my relationships. Do you remember when I had discussed having racing thoughts that would go through my head and I saw patterns of behavior towards me? This was one of the patterns. I saw that I had been treated like a slave all my life. I heard stories of how I would help my mother take care of my brothers when I was only just out of diapers myself. When I was eight, I was left to take care of both of my younger brothers while my parents worked. Between twelve and thirteen I felt like a maid, I cleaned the house daily while my parents worked. When I got married it was the same thing all over again, but at one time it became extreme when I had become a retail customer service manager and had both of my young children. My husband expected me to be "Wonder Woman." Some days I would work more than twelve hours, be expected to get the kids from daycare and then come home to cook, clean and take care of the kids. While my husband relaxed and did whatever he wanted to do.

14
Back to School

These sessions were never planned, they were all 'fly by the seat of your pants' type sessions. One of my sessions with Marsha was a guided meditation using my third eye. She said that her Master had taught her this guided meditation to view through her third eye. She said that she had altered it and found a shortcut way for herself, that she shared with her Master. This third eye experience was interesting. The intent of the third eye session was to see my past lives in which I practiced magic. The first image that came to my mind was of a Quaker woman, she had on a white bonnet. She had gray hair, a really wrinkled face, and piercing blue eyes. I thought she was rather ugly. She was in a town, or a place in which a lot of people lived and worked. She was outside, in front of her home. When I looked at her she squinted and gave me a disgusted look. The next vision felt like it was a very long time ago: I saw lush, green hills in the distance, the sky was very grey, and there was a short stone wall no more than three feet high. Then I saw him; his face was a bit hazy and it was difficult to make out his facial features. He had brown hair, brown eyes and was dressed in a robe of some sort. There were other people around and they all seemed to be very sad. There was something about to happen, like a public execution. It was a very somber vision. This man had also given me a strange look when I looked at

Master in the Making

him. I felt like he had the power to reconstruct or disguise his face so that you couldn't clearly see who he really was.

In one of the sessions with Marsha I asked her about who might be at my left arm gripping me. At this time, I had also begun to feel a grip on my right arm, so I was curious as to who or what was gripping my arms. She said that my spirit guide was on my left arm. She said that he had been my soulmate in another lifetime. We had been in love. He had only inhabited a human body once. He wasn't just a spirit guide, he was a higher-ranking spirit guide. My spirit guide is supposedly closer to god. I asked what he looked like and she said he had sandy blonde hair and brown eyes. I said, "Oh then my spirit guide is kind of cute then?" As for the gripping on my right arm, that was my Higher Self. I felt as though it was time for my Higher Self to take over care of me and to let my spirit guide rest a bit. I'm sure all that gripping my arm took a lot of energy for my spirit guide. I haven't felt my Higher Self grip my arm in a very long time. Every now and then I feel my spirit guide grip my left arm.

Some other sessions with Marsha included "EFT" which stands for Emotional Freedom Technique; others simply call it "tapping." It is a process by which one uses their hands to tap specific points on their body. It is used to move and remove trapped emotional energy in the body. This is a very physical type of therapy. I had heard of it before but hadn't tried it until then. Marsha said that she had once tapped for eight hours straight. The kind of tapping that Marsha introduced me to involved tapping the whole body not just the face or upper body. This tapping is very physical, and you can raise your heart rate and body temperature in a short time. Marsha had me try some Qigong. To me this one was a bit ridiculous. Qigong originates from China. It is an exercise with controlled breathing. The first exercise I was taught included me shaking my head from side to side, while simultaneously hitting my stomach with closed fists. This too was utilized to move energy. Then the final one I was instructed to do was to lay down with my legs in the air and feet slightly tilted as well as both hands elevated in front of my chest with my palms facing upwards. This last pose I held for about ten minutes straight.

    I was going through this program having to deal with a lot of different emotions. The diet wasn't much of a problem for me. I had already pretty much given up caffeine. I was able to have organic coffee, but I missed my creamer. I grew tired of having to drink something that tasted like dirt or drinking herbal tea every hour and a half. The routine of the schedule was the one thing that became grueling. I was giving myself 'dry brush' massages and taking baths in Himalayan bath salts for detoxing. I experienced more leg shaking. I had another set of rashes come up on my legs; one looked like a scratch mark, and a mark that looked like a welt from a belt. This rash was there for about four days. I was going through a lot. I shed nearly twenty pounds by the end. Unfortunately, I have gained it all back. I have to say that my system worked well as I did not have to open the enema kit that came in the supply box. Thank god!

    I was feeling very alone in the world. I was grieving the loss of my family again and my friends that I'd had for many years. I missed Parker. I missed being in a relationship, even if it *was* a shitty one. I was still thinking of Parker constantly. I felt more alone in the world than I ever had before, even with Shelly and the kids living with me. I felt as though I was an orphan and I had no family. I spoke to the spirit world and wanted a sign that I wasn't alone. I had no family to talk with about what I was going through. I didn't want to bug my boys, they had their own lives to live. I understood what it was like at their age and I didn't want to burden them with my problems. It did seem like I was able to see my boys a lot more once I moved to my house. Aiden and I got together almost every other week. Alex was working full time and was commuting long distance to and from work.

I had a session with Marsha in which she didn't have anything planned. She asked if there was anything that I wanted to do. Of course, I wanted to work on recalling my memories. In a prior session with Marsha she had tried to connect with my Grandfather's energy, but he didn't want to respond. She tried again in this session but couldn't connect. She said she could try to use mediumship to contact him; adding that this was very dangerous, and she had to take extra precautions to do this work. She indicated that she doesn't do this work very often because of the risk involved. I didn't want her in any danger, so I said no at first, however, I changed my mind. Marsha was able to connect with him. She said that he had never crossed over into the light and was trapped in a self-made purgatory. He had put himself in this self-made purgatory because of all the guilt and shame that he had for the things he had done. I was concerned and saddened to hear that he hadn't crossed over. I wanted him to be able to cross over to the other side. I had questions and I had a way to have them answered. I asked how old I was when he abused me? He said three. I asked if there were other times that he had abused me. Marsha timidly responded with his answer. I'm sure he had probably said something else, but I felt she tried sugar coating it for me. He had used his fingers on me several times and then decided that he could get away with what he wanted to do to me. He apologized to me for what he had done. I asked if there was anybody else that he had abused. I got five other family members names. All these family members he said he abused when they were too young to remember what had happened to them.

In the months prior to when I was realizing he had truly abused me, I had wondered if he had done anything to the animals in the basement. I had heard stories from my mother that animals were kept in the basement for slaughter. I asked about the animals. And I was sickened to find out what I had been thinking was true. My Grandfather went on and on about a family member and how physically ill they were and how worried he was about them. He wanted blessings for them. He said that this family member and I were the ones who suffered the worst of the abuse.

I wanted to know how to get my Grandfather to cross over to the other side. He wanted me to forgive him for everything and he wanted blessings for the family member. I was only willing to forgive him for what he had done to me. I didn't feel that it was my place to forgive him for *everything* that he had done. I thought about it for a few moments. I wanted him to have peace. I wanted him to cross over to the other side. I had just dealt with generational karma and my own past life karma. I thought about how my god was all forgiving and that I too should be all forgiving. I wouldn't want to be stuck in purgatory and would want somebody to forgive me, so I could move on. There was no point of him suffering any longer. I had to forgive him for everything. He was reluctant to go. He probably didn't feel worthy of being able to go into the light. Marsha and I coaxed him to. She said that his energy was vibrating at a very low rate and that it took time for his vibration to raise. She said it can be a painful process to raise your vibration in such a short period of time. It was necessary for his vibration to rise to enable him to cross over. He crossed over into the light.

Marsha called this a miracle. I never considered this a miracle and I still don't. This was a lesson in attachments. There are things in life that we hold attachments to; the things we no longer need or things that no longer serve a purpose in our lives. We cling to people, places, circumstances, situations, feelings, fears, relationships, etc. that hold us back from acquiring and achieving greater things in our lives. Once we "let go" of those things it's easier for us to move forward. By releasing and letting go in our lives, we make room for more positive to move in. I can tell you that "letting go" is not easy and it is one of my life long struggles to deal with. Letting go is my major life lesson.

I was worried about my abused family member who was ill. I hadn't spoken to this person in many years. I didn't even have a phone number to make contact. It took a little effort, but I was able to make contact. I didn't divulge that I knew that they were abused like me or that we were the ones who had suffered the worst of the abuse. I didn't want to make my family member feel uncomfortable in any way shape or form. I didn't even ask if he/she had been abused and if he/she remembered it. I told them my story. I told about having repressed memories and that I was sexually abused. I told them that my Grandfather was worried about their illness and that my Grandfather sent blessings. My family member sat and listened to this story and didn't say anything. I asked about any illness and he/she said they did not disclose any illness to me. I was a little disappointed about not having confirmation about an illness. I figured that I had just dumped this crazy story in his/her lap and needed time to digest what I had just said. Since no illness was validated, I suggested a visit to the doctor for a checkup. Several weeks later I got a message stating that he/she had been to the doctor, altered their diet and was feeling a lot better. I was happy to hear this news. This gave me some validation that I truly did communicate with my Grandfather on the other side.

While working with Kathryn, we discussed that I had issues with women. We discussed my relationships with the other women who had been in my life. Women that I had issues with. I brought up Devlin and asked her what that relationship was all about. I asked if Devlin was just jealous of me or if she wanted to be me. She said no, she was in love with you and when you figured it all out, it totally freaked you out. To say the least.

I would have rather had a male friend over a female friend any day. I have had the perception that women are catty, backstabbing and unreliable. Whereas with a guy, from my viewpoint is WYSIWYG (What you see is what you get). Issues with women are tied to femininity and the ability to be emotionally expressive. Kathryn did her thing and was looking at the energies surrounding me. She picked up on secrets; more to the point, sexual secrets. There was a lot of sexual secrets surrounding me that came from my family, associated with guilt and shame. Kathryn said she was having a lot of my ancestors surrounding her and wanting to talk with me. She said that there's a man here who wants to talk with you. He has gray hair, a beard and a mustache. He's coming through on your mother's side. I didn't know anybody on my mother's side who fit that description; it did however cross my mind that it might have been my Uncle Joe. She asked if my mother was a party girl. I said I guess she was from the stories I had heard. Kathryn said she could see some sort of club, membership, organization or a fraternal organization. That set off a light bulb in my head. When I was taking care of my Grandmother Marjorie, she had told the caregiver stories of being in a sisterhood organization that was connected to this fraternal organization. My Grandmother had told this caregiver stories of Joe's first wife Bonnie and her doing some crazy things while they belonged to this sisterhood. I asked if it was Joe and wondered why he showed up on my mother's side, rather than my father's side. It was Joe.

    Joe was one of my favorite relatives to be around. My dad would always get him to tell stories. He was able to tell made up stories like they truly happened. The prompt my dad would use with Joe was: "There I was forty thousand feet in the air…" I was happy to hear from him. Kathryn said he came to tell me a story, so I said: "So there I was forty thousand feet in the air…" This wasn't one of those types of stories and he had a seriousness to him. He said that he saw how the women in my family were treated and he didn't like it. The women in my family were all subservient to the men and were treated poorly. Kathryn was seeing and probably hearing Joe tell her this story; as she was telling me. My Grandmother and Bonnie had participated in a type of "prostitution" or a type of "sexual slavery" that was connected to this secretive fraternal organization. I had heard stories over the years, and it wasn't just from my Grandmother's caregiver. I wasn't shocked to hear these stories about my Grandmother. I had somehow heard that my dad was very young and had caught my Grandmother in the backseat with a man.

    I was trying to figure out how old my dad was at the time. My Grandmother had divorced my biological Grandfather, within a year of my dad being born. That's a story within itself. I never had met my dad's dad, but I knew that the man died of a broken heart. He loved my Grandmother and she shut him out. My Grandmother said that my Grandfather had suffered from mental illness. My dad's dad had served as a "frog man" in World War II. What I had heard was that he had been shot in the leg in the battle of Iwo Jima and received a Purple Heart. My Grandmother remarried Rudy in the year 1955. Joe is Rudy's brother. I recall hearing stories of my Grandmother and Rudy taking my dad to Disneyland the first week they opened the park in July of 1955. My dad was eight years old when Disneyland opened. I couldn't image that my Grandmother would have been behaving that way after marrying Rudy. My dad could have been seven years old. My dad's birthday is in the later part of January and Marjorie and Rudy weren't married until Valentine's Day of 1955.

    Uncle Joe said that my dad was forced to go to one of the fraternal organization's meetings and be part of a "rite of passage". Joe said that he knew of it and that he didn't want anything to do with it. Although he knew about it, he did nothing to stop it. He said that after my dad had gone to this "rite of passage" he never told anybody about it and he was never the same after it. It had changed my dad forever. Kathryn said she was seeing the scene in which my dad's "rite of passage" took place. She said that there were naked women with their hands tied behind their back and naked men. The women were performing oral copulation on the men. She said my dad was there in that room. Kathryn didn't tell me what happened in that "rite of passage", nor did I ask. I think the point was to let me know that my dad had been sexually abused as well. It didn't matter how he was sexually abused. Just by taking him there and exposing him to that was sexual abuse. I had forgotten about Joe being present and asked Kathryn to ask him if he needed anything from me. He didn't need anything from me. His response was "I thought we were family?" And I said "Yes, we are family and thank you Joe." To this day I still cry about Uncle Joe telling me we are family. He was my Step Uncle, but he was my Uncle, just as his brother Rudy was my Grandfather and I didn't consider him my Step Grandfather. Rudy was my Grandfather in every sense. I think Joe knew that I needed to know that I had some family around me. He told me that they were always around me. It's not coincidental that the only large family photo that I had with me wasn't even that of my own families. It was Joe, Rudy, their sister Miriam and brother John with their mother. They were all young teenagers in the photo. I had ended up with this photo after my Grandparents had passed. I had always wanted to send it to John's daughter Karen, but I never got around to it. I

Master in the Making

decided that I needed that photo now. I framed the picture and now have it hanging in my family room.

Both Marsha and Kathryn were giving me titles of books to read. I really didn't want to read any books, nor did I want to listen to any audiobooks. I was given an assignment to watch "Awake: The Life of Yogananda." I did watch it. I found it very interesting that science is so interested in spirituality. I had a hard time watching it, from the perspective of seeing these people give up their lives to follow this man and hang on his every word. *That* I have an issue with; following somebody. It is how I have lived my entire life and I detest it. I have a problem with the concept of a modern-day guru. Marsha had once proclaimed that she aspired to become a saint. I find this stuff to be so egotistical. Marsha had many times praised her Master, and the way she talked about him was just fanatical to me. To me it felt very cultish. Maybe this was why I did not want to read the books that they had suggested to me. I didn't want to have my beliefs and thoughts influenced by them or their books. Even so, I must admit I had thoughts of moving to Taos and working alongside Marsha and Kathryn. I did think about having them as my masters, but my views on that were changing.

I was feeling that God was pulling me closer towards him and he was asking me to follow a path and have faith in it. I knew I was learning lessons even if I wasn't getting all the answers to my questions. I knew he wanted me to become a spiritual healer. I knew that he wanted me to write a book about my experiences. I got the impression he wanted me to speak out and write about sexual abuse. When I had read "Repressed Memories: A Journey to Recovery from

Master in the Making

Childhood Sexual Abuse," I had done some research on the statistics of sexual abuse. The numbers were staggering. I had gotten the notion that those numbers weren't exactly true. I figured a truer figure would be much higher because of my story and others like mine. I thought that God may have been calling me for more than just to speak out about child sexual abuse. I thought that there was another message that he wanted me to convey to the world. I am still not clear on what he wants me to do. I had questioned myself on whether I wanted to continue to take this path and move forward with what God was asking of me. God suggested that I really think about everything and mull it over. I was afraid of having to give things up. I was afraid that it meant living this holy and pure life. I understand now that he wanted me because I am not perfect and holy as I am. He wanted me because of me, because of who I am. I do know that other people who feel this call also feel that they are special. I felt like I was "the chosen one" or "the golden child" at times. I keep telling my ego it's very full of itself and that a lot of people go through a period of feeling this way. In the end I was feeling urged by God to tell my story even if I didn't fully understand why.

    I still had a couple more sessions to go with Marsha and Kathryn. The following session I had with Marsha she wanted to balance my feminine/masculine energies in my body. I laid down on my bed. I put my phone to the side, so I could still hear her. I felt her move my right leg and I saw it move. I closed my eyes and she started calling on the vibration of unconditional love to surround us and disinvited any negative energies. She called upon four Ascended Masters. The name of the first one, I cannot remember their name. I felt his energy to my right side. He was followed by Osho, Yogananda and then Jesus Christ. I felt each one's energy as they entered. When Yogananda entered I felt a very strong energy, it was almost overwhelming. Then I heard her call upon Jesus Christ, and I thought for sure that it would be stronger and bolder than that of Yogananda, but it wasn't. Jesus Christ had a very soft flowy type of energy. She called upon them to come and heal me. She asked they heal my eyes, my brain, my heart, my hands and some other things. I was emotionally overwhelmed with what I was experiencing. She said that Jesus Christ had a message for me. He wanted to give me a prayer to say. He said that I had free will and that it was up to me whether I wanted to say the prayer. I lost it right then and there. Jesus knows me. He knew that I'm a big fan of "free will." I was sobbing. "If you want an ego male pray for an ego male. If you want a divine male pray for a divine male. Pray that you will know the difference between them. Julie, you are too tough on yourself. You need to take it easier on Julie." I sobbed even harder when he said to take it easier on Julie. It's so true that I am very hard on myself.

I have forgotten what was said word for word. This is the gist of it. I know what an ego male is and have had plenty of experience with that in my life. I have never known a divine man and I have prayed for one. What more can I say? It was an experience that Jesus Christ was here giving me a prayer to say. Interesting. Oh, by the way, you might be wondering why Jesus Christ is considered an Ascended Master vs. an Archangel. Archangels typically have not inhabited a human body and Ascended Masters have inhabited a human body.

Master in the Making

My next session with Kathryn I asked about my Great Grandfather Larry. He had been on my mind the past couple of days. I wanted to know if he was still roaming around the Earth and why he hadn't crossed over. He almost instantly appeared to Kathryn's right side. Of course, Kathryn was acting as a medium between us. I can't remember exactly how the conversation had started. She said that he had another child before he had my Grandmother Marjorie. This was shocking. He had another child when he was in the Navy on the U.S.S. Arizona. He had lied about his age to get into the service. He was very young. Kathryn was able to pick up some visions of this. She said that the child he had prior was either a Hispanic or black baby girl. It was very taboo in those days. He didn't treat the mother of the child very well. He did love her, but he treated her as though she was a slave. I knew that my Great Grandfather Larry had belonged to the fraternal organization that my Grandmother Marjorie was connected to through the sisterhood. Marjorie was a type of a legacy member. After my Great Grandmother Gladys had passed, Marjorie had my mother and I come over and go through closets. I came across some business cards and pieces of paper that had been Larry's. In those papers were indications that Larry could have possibly belonged to the Ku Klux Klan. There were cards that read "white members only" and "no blacks." I knew to a degree that Larry had been racist, so it was a little shocking to hear he had another child and one of color.

Larry had his own attachment that kept him trapped here. His attachment was that he wanted somebody to know that he had this other child. Nobody knew that this child existed until now. He wanted his family to know that this child existed. He said he wanted us to find her. I'm not sure if he was aware of how much time had passed since he died, because that woman was probably more than likely dead and gone. He knew that she had probably lived a life of struggle and strife. I didn't want to explain to him that I was no longer talking to anybody in my family, but I promised him that I would make it known that he had another daughter. I wanted to see him cross over into the light as well.

    I'm not sure if I had asked about the experience I had in his room when I was little or not. I'm not sure how Kathryn told me that he had hidden a document. The document had to do with the birth of that child. Like a birth certificate. He hid the document in the wall of his old upstairs bedroom. The very bedroom I had my very first encounter with him from the other side. In that very spot that I felt him, and my son Alex had felt a creepy sensation. In the very house that my parents, brothers and sister-in-law are living in today. I texted Greg to let him know that there were documents hidden in the wall. I told him exactly where the spot was. My intuition told me where to find the documents. To the left of the closet about five to six feet from the floor and inside the wall. I didn't think that it was very hard to get to. It's nearly a year later and my family has not been curious enough to retrieve that from the wall. Let me tell you, if I had access to get to into the attic and retrieve it myself - I would have done so already. It's a piece of my family and a piece of my family history. I would have already found my Great Aunt on a genealogy website by now and I would have had more validation about having had a conversation with my Great Grandfather Larry.

Master in the Making

I had to promise Larry that I would tell the others and try to find his other daughter. He too crossed over into the light. Kathryn said that he had his Navy uniform on and proudly saluted and walked over to the other side. He seemed proud to have served in the service. I think that was probably a very good time in his life. Growing up I heard stories of him running away from home. He rode the rails and took the name "Casey Jones." I think he ran away from home because of his strict oppressive religious upbringing. I could see where a teenager would rebel against that kind of oppression and run away. I know that he had the family karmas of "stubbornness" in him and the "power through the end to get a task complete." Isn't that what he did in the end? He was stubborn about leaving without completing his task of letting somebody know that he had another daughter.

My last session with Kathryn was back to my issues. I had issues with creating good boundaries with people and relationships. I had problems being submissive and negotiating terms. I didn't want to be told what to do and I still don't. I had issues with having to be right in an argument. I needed to appeal to the needs of others to negotiate. I hated negotiating. I felt awkward in that position, because I was afraid to push my limits and ask for what I wanted and needed. It's not that I hadn't done this in the past, it's that I wasn't consistent once the terms were spelled out. I had issues with holding others accountable for the terms that they had agreed upon. I felt that I had to suffer, go without and be the giver. I had associated being a taker as being a bad person. I had sacrificed myself in the process of this way of thinking. I had to work on taking with integrity and taking graciously. I had to learn how to honor somebody else when I was a taker and determine what I was taking and why I was taking it. I still have some things to work on from that session.

My last session with Marsha was interesting, like all of them. This one we did another guided third eye meditation. This time I was to ask three questions, anything I wanted to ask. I still had Parker on my mind. I asked if he really did love me. I was prepared to see anything. I saw his face he was crying. He was lit up with a brilliant white light, so bright it looked like he was wearing a white t-shirt. He doesn't own any white t-shirts. I interpreted that the white light was the love he had felt for me. I felt his chest aching for me and his stomach hurt. I felt so bad. I had broken his heart. I sobbed and said, "oh my god". The second question was if my mother would ever believe me and find it in her heart to be sympathetic toward me for what had happened to me. I was prepared to see anything I saw. I saw my mother in her dining room and we were sitting down at the table. We were sitting down to talk about her not believing what happened to me and wanting to have proof of it. I don't remember her say anything. I could read the expression on her face. She wasn't going to believe me with or without proof. She was never going to change her position or stance on the subject. I couldn't think of a third question to ask.

Marsha asked what I had asked. I didn't really want to share it with her and can't remember if I had. I know that I had asked her if Parker had been my soulmate. She had me say his name three times and she was able to see. She said that we have had two or three other lifetimes together. We were soulmates and we had a sacred love. Sacred love is one of unconditional love. Sacred love is also a connection to another person on a mental, emotional, physical and spiritual level. Now I understood why I had felt that he and I were soulmates. Now I knew why I have had such a hard time getting over him. It wasn't just about this lifetime and the relationship we had in this lifetime. I didn't feel so bad now for not getting over him, like I thought I should have. I learned that you aren't always meant to be with your soulmate forever. I was lucky to have found one and spent some time with them for a little while. Some people never know that love and some don't believe that kind of love exists.

    Marsha, Kathryn and I were going to go on a soul retrieval in a few days. I was driving out to Taos by myself. Marsha said that we were going to do a fire ceremony. She informed me that I should bring anything that I wanted to burn, and "let go" of it. I don't think I was truly ready to let go of Parker, especially after having just found out that he really had been my soulmate. I was planning on taking some socks Parker had given me for Christmas. To me they were ugly Christmas socks. I couldn't bear to look at them as they would only remind me of him. He never gave me much of anything. He didn't give me any letters or cards, ever. We never took any photos together. The only thing I had, that I could "let go" of was the stupid ass socks. I told Marsha that I intended on writing a letter to Devlin, so that I could let go of the anger I still held towards her. I had also been kicking around the idea of giving up smoking but didn't say anything to Marsha about it.

    The next day I left early in the morning. I played a lot of music and did so much singing that I was hoarse. I stopped at rest stops along the way. I started seeing Ravens at these rest stops. That night I stayed in Flagstaff. I had gone outside my hotel room to call Shelly and let her know I arrived at my hotel. As I was walking around the corner from my hotel there was a glassblowing shop and through that window, I saw several Ravens. The next morning, I was awoken by what sounded like, you guessed it folks, Ravens! When I went down to get some coffee and to have a cigarette, guess what I saw! Those Ravens that had woken me up. They were huge. They had to have stood at least two feet tall. Of course, I had to google the symbolism of the Raven! Duh! Go google for yourself, because there are many different meanings and significance around this smart bird.

I was back on the road for the last stretch of highway to Taos. I had joked with friends that I was going to do "Jedi Training in the desert, because the force is strong with this one." While driving, I thought about writing this book that you are reading. I thought about the title and chapter names. There was so much I had to say in this book. I cried all the way to Taos thinking of how I broke Parker's heart and just how much he did love me. I loved him just as much. I hurt just as much as he hurt in the vision I had seen. That evening I met Marsha and Kathryn at their shop at six. We loaded up our backpacks and sleeping bags into Kathryn's Toyota Landcruiser. I was about to embark on an eighteen-hour fasting journey into the desert. We drove a short distance down the highway and then onto a dirt road into the desert. Kathryn and Marsha made small talk and I listened. Marsha was talking about her intuitive training seminar. She had invited me to go and I told her that I needed to give it some thought. She had been talking about one of her students she recently had and how he picked up on that she had a cat. She said that he was also able to intuitively see that her roommate was abusing her cat while she was gone. One of the things that had stood out in my mind about this conversation between the two of them was that Marsha had a roommate. I started doing the math in my head. If Kathryn and Marsha own the shop and work the hours that they say they do, (It's a math word problem, remember them from school?) I figured that the shop had to bring in somewhere in the ballpark of three hundred thousand dollars a year. We then subtract labor, product, overhead, taxes, etc. Let's say they take home eighty-five thousand each. Why does she have a roommate? It wasn't making sense to me.

Driving for nearly an hour, we had made many turns on these dusty, bumpy dirt roads. The sun had gone down. We had passed a group of men as we approached our destination, and Kathryn and Marsha seemed a little nervous by their presence. For some reason I didn't mind their presence at all; we had passed many campers along our way on these roads. Coming to the end of the road, we parked. We each grabbed our gear and started walking on a dirt path. At first, we went downhill and then it leveled off for a while. Then the path went up and got rocky. I was breathing heavy. It was a full moon, but we still needed a flashlight to see our path. I couldn't really see where this path was in the larger surrounding landscape. We came up and around the side of a mountain. We were on a cliff. Marsha was asking me to jump or put my foot on this ledge to get over to the cave. I am deathly afraid of heights and this was pushing my limits. I'm not really a hiker, let alone a mountain climber. I get anxiety just driving near large cliffs. I was full of anxiety, so I had to figure out another way to get into the cave. There was another large rock below the ledge. I was able to sit on my butt and crab walk to the opening of the cave. There was some level land in front of the cave, but not much. The cave was big. The inside dimensions were probably fifteen feet deep, twenty feet wide and at least ten feet tall. There was a small circle of rocks where others had fires. It reminded me of the Flintstones; it even had a window on one side. The cave face was wide open but had a small man-made rock barrier along the bottom. Marsha explained that the cave was a sacred Native American cave and used for "rites of passage" ceremonies and rituals.

    Marsha had brought some Duraflame logs with her. I was relieved that she brought wood. It had crossed my mind that I might be made to go get wood as part of my "training." Marsha kept referring to this "soul retrieval" as "training." Before the trip out to Taos I had asked her what we would be doing. The only thing I really got out of her was the fire ceremony and "training." She said spirit would guide the night. The cave needed to be prepared before we began. Marsha had taken some Palo Santo out of her backpack. She lit three sticks and handed one to Kathryn and one to me. I had never used Palo Santo. I had only used white sage smudge sticks. The Palo Santo did not want to stay lit. The three of us kept blowing on our sticks to keep it lit, so that we could walk around the wall of the cave for the Palo Santo smoke to cleanse and bless the area.

    We sat down by the fire after cleansing and blessing the cave. I was asked what I wanted out of the soul retrieval. I can't remember exactly what I had said, but it was something to the effect of wanting to have healing of the emotional and mental trauma I had suffered as a child. I also wanted to "let go" of Parker and Devlin. From there I was asked to go get the things that I wanted to burn in the fire ceremony. I got the socks that Parker had given me, the letter I wrote Devlin and my pack of cigarettes. They had no idea that I was bringing socks or cigarettes. Kathryn started the ceremony with us gazing into the fire and meditating on her words. Then I put Parker's socks in the fire. Marsha proceeded with the ritual with intention for Parker to be banished from my life for good. Inside I didn't want that at all. I still wanted to be friends with him. My heart was still aching for him and wanted him in my life. My head said I should let him go. I wanted Marsha to change her intention right then and there, because I didn't agree with what she had said. I had a much easier time putting Devlin's letter in the fire and I finally was feeling free of all my anger toward her. Now, I half-heartedly put my remaining two cigarettes into the fire.

This all happened nearly a year ago and I still occasionally hear from Parker. He texted me a couple of days ago and I called him. I never know if it's going to be the last time that he contacts me. He said to me: "you deserve better." I said: "I know, that's why I had to let you go." I told him if he stopped chasing women and quit drinking then maybe. Conversations with him are always brief, when we went to say goodbye, I told him I loved him, and he said he loved me too. I have been smoking like a chimney writing this book, so there's part of the results of the fire ceremony for you!

Master in the Making

Kathryn had me stand up and face her. We started off with Qigong[2], the exercise where we shake our heads side to side and hit our stomach with both our fists. Marsha was behind me beating a drum and chanting. We started tapping. I don't know for how long. The tapping got more intense and so did the drumming and chanting. Marsha was tapping on my backside and I was tapping on my front side. Marsha instructed me to scream with her. We did this several times, because I wasn't screaming loud enough. Kathryn came up to me and said Marsha is getting frustrated you need to put everything into screaming and repeat every word that Marsha says even if you don't believe it or feel it. We made a couple more attempts. I screamed louder than before. I repeated the words she said, "I hate you mom! You're a fucking bitch!" I wasn't connecting with these words, because I didn't feel this way. I collapsed to my knees and threw dirt around the cave to act out how angry I was supposed to be at my mother. Once I did this correctly, Marsha and Kathryn verbally guided me to my three-year-old self. I had to go retrieve little Julie. I had to save her and protect her and never let her go. I had to promise her that I wouldn't let anybody hurt her every again. I had tried this exercise before when I had read: "Repressed Memories: A Journey to Recovery from Childhood Sexual Abuse." I was never able to get little Julie to come with me. She was very angry and stubborn, she didn't trust me. This time she came with me. She gave me a big hug and wouldn't let go. One

---

[2] True meaning of Qigong: Qi gong, chi kung, or chi gung is a holistic system of slow, coordinated body posture and movement, breathing, and meditation used in the belief that it promotes health, spirituality, and martial arts training.

day when I started writing this book, I felt her come up to me and hug and kiss me. She was happy about what I was doing.

When I got up from the cave floor, I think we did some more tapping and more Qigong. Kathryn was asking what I was feeling. I was feeling sick and was physically reacting as though I was sick. I was dry heaving without anything coming up. It was strange because I saw and felt Kathryn having the same experience as me. She was dry heaving and feeling sick too. Her reactions seemed to happen to her seconds before they happened to me. I felt like thousands of tiny pins were rising from my belly and coming up to my throat. I don't know how long this went on, but after a while it subsided. We took a break at that point. I thought that I would see what they were focused on in their mind's eye, but I had no visions or inkling to what they were doing with their spiritual gifts. Personally, I wasn't seeing how this was "training." At some point my quest had changed from a soul retrieval and getting my memories; to a quest to becoming enlightened.

We had laid out our sleeping bags in a row right next to each other inside the cave. Mine was in the middle. I sat there drinking some water during a break. Marsha came over to me and told me we were going to do the other Qigong exercise, the one with our legs and hands in the air. She said before we start you have three choices and with those choices you will be rewarded accordingly. The first option was to do the pose for twenty minutes and I would be given a little information. The second option was to do it for forty minutes and I would be given even more information. The third option was to do the pose for one hour and I would be given all the information I wanted. I chose the third option. We all laid there doing the pose for an hour. Kathryn fell asleep, which is kind of unbelievable considering that the pose requires some focus and keeping your legs up in the air. I really can't believe I had done that for a whole hour. I had these cute little mittens on and that was my focus. The mittens were so soft, cute and I loved them. The hour was up, and I put my legs down then my legs started shaking. They shook like they had before, but this was more intense than ever, and it lasted a lot longer. Kathryn and Marsha were outside the cave sitting on a rock in the moonlight. They told me to come out and soak up the moonlight. I couldn't really sit. My legs were still shaking. I laid there with my feet on the rock. I had to just let my legs shake. I forgot to ask what information I would get. I was still waiting to see visions of what they were doing mentally with their gifts. I didn't see or hear anything.

Kathryn and Marsha went back into the cave. I had seen the steep cliff that we were on and it caused me some anxiety. I had to pee, so I waited until Kathryn and Marsha went back into the cave. Suddenly, I was on the ground. I couldn't get up. I felt paralyzed. I was panicking. I had never in my life felt this. I called out to them and told them, "I think I am having a panic attack." I could hear the two of them talking to each other. Kathryn said I think you need to go get her. Marsha helped me up off the ground outside the cave. I wasn't feeling well. It was time to lay down and go to sleep for a little while. We all got into our sleeping bags. My stomach started hurting bad. It felt like sharp needles gouging my insides. Kathryn said she could feel my pain. I asked what it was. She said it was from abandonment and

Master in the Making

anger. She said she had never felt such pain in her entire life. I laid there in my sleeping bag trying to relax, but in excruciating pain. I felt something poke my leg. It freaked me out, because there are scorpions and big spiders in the desert. I sat up and was trying to see if there was anything there. It felt like I had a stinger on my knee. Marsha grabbed her small flashlight and was trying to pull out whatever it was. I let out a yelp and told her I hadn't shaved, and she was pulling my leg hair. Later, I determined that I had brushed a cactus with my sleeping bag and a needle got stuck in it. My stomach was still hurting. Marsha had put some music on, so I was trying to focus on the music. Marsha asked if I wanted her to spoon me to comfort me. I said okay. She asked if I wanted her to rub the pain and I said okay. She knew exactly where my pain was. She was feeling my pain too. My pain even moved, and she was able to know that my pain moved. As I was listening to the music, I was getting emotional from the lyrics and she picked up on that. She asked if I wanted her to change the music. I fell asleep.

When I woke up, I was the only one awake. Marsha had woken up and told me to wake her up right before sunrise. As the sky slowly got lighter and lighter out, I could see how we came in the night before. I started getting anxiety about how I was going to get out of there. I was thinking helicopter. I woke up Marsha and Kathryn as the sun rose. I was still sitting on my sleeping bag. They must have been looking elsewhere, but I was looking straight out of the cave and saw two Ravens fly by. Marsha turned and was looking out of the cave when a third Raven flew by and she said: "Oh look, there's a Raven." I do believe that the Raven was my power animal on that trip.

Master in the Making

We began packing our things up. Marsha had wanted us to finish our ceremony on top of the cave, but I refused. I made it very clear that there was no way I was climbing up on top of that cave. I wasn't sure how I was going to get out of the desert. I had to ask them for help to guide me out of there. Sometime during our rituals, the night before, Kathryn had told me that I had to ask for help when I needed, and that although I had endurance, I lacked discipline. I know she had been right about needing to ask for help. They made me scream and breathe in and out all the way around that cliff bend. I had anxiety the entire way. I was petrified. Obviously, I made it out; I'm here writing about it. We made the hike out of the desert. The hike was at least thirty minutes. We loaded our things up and before leaving Marsha took a selfie of the three of us. There was a big white beam of light coming from the top of my head and extending into the sky.

We made our way back down that dirt road back to the highway. We were not done. Marsha had to think of another place to go that she considered sacred like the cave we were at. We were back on the highway. They really didn't know where to go. We were on dirt roads again. The two of them had been carrying on a conversation the whole time. As we were approaching a place that Marsha was telling Kathryn to park, I heard Native Americans chanting in my head. I thought to myself, this is it. You're crazy, you have completely lost your mind now. Out of all the crazy things I had experienced in the past few months, this was the one that made me think I had completely lost it. I did hear Native American chanting. The Native Americans who had performed ceremonies in that sacred cave and the ones who achieved the "rite of passage" had come to signal to me that I too had achieved the "rite of passage."

Kathryn grabbed a yoga mat out of her truck and we made our way to an area where flood water had left a ditch. The three of us went down into the ditch. I laid down on the mat. The rituals that had been performed the night before were to release negative energy. The rituals that they were about to perform on me in that ditch were to fill me up with positive energy. Marsha had said an opening prayer. She proceeded to shout positive affirmations. She was very close to my left leg; I could feel her breath; I could feel the vibration of her words. She shouted "Julie is awesome! Julie is great! I love you Julie!" I felt Kathryn touch my hands and different spots and then she had her hands over my stomach area. She didn't touch me. She was pushing energy into me. I was in pain. The pain was shearing. I was crying. She kept pushing the energy into me. The pain was as bad or worse than the night before. At one point I had to grab her hands and told her that it hurt. Kathryn continued as Marsha continued to shout into my left leg. The pain subsided, and both stopped their rituals. Marsha looked at me and said: "God has been calling you for a long time." I said I know he has. I wasn't trying to be a bitch or anything. It was just something I had known. I knew God was calling me to do something.

Our ceremonies and rituals weren't done yet. She said that we needed to let the universe know that I was "reborn." She said that we need to move the positive energy around inside me. We had more Qigong to do. The three of us were in a circle shaking our heads side to side and punching our stomachs with our fists. We looked disheveled and were dirty from the last eighteen hours in the desert. We were screaming again. This time I had to scream: "I'm free." She wanted me to scream louder and was telling me to do so. Just then, to the right of me about thirty yards away, a blue jeep with its windows rolled down and four guys inside were driving by. One of the passengers called out: "Hey look, Witch Women!" I giggled and said, "And yes, we are in our native habitat." It was odd that these two women didn't laugh. I mean really, you must admit what had just taken place was very funny. The whole scene was funny. I wondered how often people came across witches in the desert. It must have happened often enough in Taos for these guys to know that we were witches.

    I continued to scream until Marsha was satisfied. Marsha had picked up a pinkish heart-shaped rock from the ground when we had first gotten to this location. I'm pretty sure that she made this part up on the fly. I had to pick a spot to mark where I had been "reborn." I picked a lush green pine tree. Marsha gave me the rock. I found a stick, dug a hole and buried the pink heart-shaped rock under the tree. Marsha handed me a stick and told me that it was my first wand. It was a fragile twig. (I kept it, but a few months later, it had gotten broken and I threw it away.) She marked the location in Google maps and sent it to me. She said, that if I needed to get more of my energy, I knew where to find it.

    On the way back to the shop, they took me out to eat. It was a cool and funky vegan restaurant. All the seating was outside in what looked like somebody's backyard. Hammocks, hanging chairs and yard decor hung from the trees. The food and drink were good. We sat there and made chit chat about the night before. I looked at Marsha and asked: "Did my virginity grow back?" She looked at me and started replying very seriously. I don't remember what Marsha said, but she thought I was serious. Omg. I let her off the hook. "I'm only kidding." Kathryn laughed at that one, because she knew I didn't really think that it was possible. I felt as though Marsha thought I was this innocent that I didn't know much. She had treated me that way throughout the entire time we had done the counseling sessions. She's not the only one who had treated me as though I was innocent and naive. I got that a lot from people in my life.

We were done, and I was free. The first thing I did was find a gas station to buy some cigarettes and a lighter. I went to my hotel to see if I could check in early. They were so accommodating, it makes me want to go back there again. They had housekeeping clean my room next, so that I could get into my room and relax. I checked in with Shelly to let her know I was alive, well and coming back the next day. I went and got McDonald's and watched Star Trek. There was a wedding there that night. It was a little noisy with a live band playing, but I was able to sleep through the night. I got up early the next morning and got back on the road.

As I was driving, I got a couple of calls. One of my friends checking in with me to make sure that I was okay. Another one was from a client. We talked for well over an hour. I told him what I was up to. It had been a couple months since we had spoken. He called me about the title on his house and wanting to change it. I think he used that as an excuse to ask me to reach out to his wife who had been acting odd. She had been hospitalized and given a new medication. He said that the medication caused a personality change in her and he was afraid of losing his wife. I promised I would try to get together with his wife for lunch at minimum. It wasn't the first time a client had called me on the premise of real estate. Real estate was not the reason they call me. One client found out that I was single and called to ask me out. The thing is about this phone call while I was on the road, is that I did a lot of talking myself. I told him how I was going to become a "spiritual healer." I told him that I was going to write a book about all my experiences over the past few months. It also made me think of an awful story his wife had told me. Her daughter had been sexually abused by her Grandfather. How she found out that her daughter had been sexually abused was when she went to give her daughter a bath. The daughter screamed bloody murder from the soapy water in the bathtub. It made me start thinking about what signs I might have shown after I had been sexually abused. Why hadn't anybody picked up any signs of it? Why hadn't my mother picked up anything about it afterwards? I could only imagine that I hadn't acted like myself afterwards.

    With so many hours on the road, my attention turned back to Parker. I missed him so. I hadn't seen him in eight months. We had only dated for seven months. I had intentions of going by his house on my way home. I made my way into his mobile home park and he wasn't home. I was a little heartbroken to see his car gone. I wanted to tell him about everything I had just learned about us. How it makes perfect sense that the reason we couldn't get over each other was that we were soulmates.

    A few days after returning from Taos, I left to see my sister Tara in Oregon. I hadn't seen her in twenty-two years. She lived on a big piece of property with her longtime boyfriend. She had taken me into town to a spiritual bookstore. I felt like we had finally really started establishing a relationship with one another. I needed somebody in my life who I could call family. Even though I had Uncle Joe and my family in the spiritual world, I needed a physical person I could connect with as a family member. I feel we have more in common than we don't, even though we weren't raised together. In one of my sessions with Kathryn I had asked about the relationship with my sister. She said that she's your twin and that she's more from outer space and I am earthier. We have many things in common. Over the past year and even more recently, I see that we are. Tara speaks with a different vocabulary than I, but we are usually on the same page about what we are talking about.

When I returned from Oregon, I had texted Parker that I was going to write a book. I told him I had wanted to meet with him and talk. Parker had "pulled my ponytail" for months about getting together. I didn't think it would happen. He called me and told me to come get him. I was shocked that we were going to see each other again after eight months. We went to the Dust Bowl for lunch and we reminisced about being there when we dated. I knew he felt the same way I had about the place when we were dating, but I had never heard him express it to me. He talked like he wanted to get back together. I still loved him, and he still loved me; when we dated, we were best friends. He told me he could still give me drum lessons. I told him that he was an awesome drummer, but he had no patience to be a drum teacher. It was nice of him to offer.

I told him that I had found out that we were soulmates and that we had shared a few other lifetimes together. I told him that it made sense to me now. He believed in the supernatural too. He had his own experiences. When he was little, he had seen three jinn hover over his bed. His mother had also taught him how to cast spells. He told me he had wished his ex-wife dead and she recently had suffered a stroke. He said he had wished his sister dead and she had been diagnosed with serious illness. I told him that he shouldn't do that, because karma is a serious bitch to mess with. I asked if he wished those kinds of things on me. I asked him not to. He said he never wished anything bad on me and he would never do that to me. When we were dating, he would tell me that I deserve better and wished that I would meet a good man, a rich man, a man that would take care of me. I know he knows that he could never give me what I want or deserve in a relationship. It just wasn't going to happen for us. I was just happy that afternoon being able to hang out with my best friend for a little while. I still wasn't over him. It was going to take almost another year to heal my heartache.

  One afternoon I was lying in my bed reflecting on everything I had experienced. I was missing Parker again. I was thinking about writing my book. I felt an energy sensation. I had been feeling energy movement inside me for a couple months now and I knew what it felt like. This time the energy sensation was different. It felt as though somebody was tying four cords to my belly button. I sensed it was Marsha. I had my reservations about working with these people anymore. I had made my mind up that I wasn't going to the intuitive seminar, nor was I going to move there and work alongside them in their shop. I wasn't about to spend more money on something that I would feel like I didn't get anything out of. I was feeling that I hadn't gotten much out of my trip to Taos. I had a lot more questions and felt a little spiritually abused by Marsha and Kathryn. I hadn't retrieved my memories. I wanted my questions answered. I felt that the soul retrieval I got wasn't authentic like the ones I had read about or the videos I had watched online. I wanted to know what they did during my soul retrieval. I wanted to know what they intuitively saw when they were doing their spiritual work on me. I felt short changed and taken advantage of. I texted Marsha and Kathryn about this. Marsha set up a session for us to meet.

Marsha Face-Timed me. I felt like she was giving me the run around. I asked her about the energy sensation with the cords. She gave me an unsatisfying answer. I felt she was giving me a song and dance. I sensed she was lying to me and was trying to cover up what she had done. What I have read and know about cords is that they are created naturally and organically. You shouldn't feel cords being attached. I did a few rituals to cut the cords.

Marsha's behavior, not just then, but from the beginning, had reminded me of Devlin. Marsha wanted to tell me what to do and how to do it. She thought I was naive like Devlin thought I was naive. I began to draw parallels between the two of them and the situations. I wasn't buying what Marsha was selling me. On top of that, during our Face-Time conversation when I asked about my memories, she brought up her sexual abuse story again. The whole conversation had me irritated and pissed off at her. I was pissed off at myself too for having done the soul retrieval. Marsha had told me on more than one occasion that I had been very abused and neglected as a child. I sensed that there was more that I didn't know. The wheels in my mind had started to turn wildly. I wanted the questions about my soul retrieval answered. Now I wanted answers to all the new questions I had about being abused and neglected as a child.

I mean I had all kinds of questions running through my head from Marsha saying that I was very abused and neglected as a child. I mean think about it. I had repressed memories of my sexual abuse. What else had happened to me? Could I possibly have more repressed memories? Was I sexually abused by anybody else? Was there child pornography out there of me? Was I prostituted out? Was I drugged as a child? I mean some crazy shit goes through your mind when you are told that you were very abused and neglected as a child. I came up with a very long list of questions and emailed it to both Kathryn and Marsha. They decided that it would be best if we set up a Face-Time session. They knew I was pissed off. They knew that maybe they hadn't debriefed me properly after the soul retrieval. I still owed them money for the soul retrieval. In my mind I wasn't going to pay them until I had my questions answered. I was so upset about all of this that I had completely missed a day of work. It wasn't like me to just not show up at work. (I hadn't realized that I had even missed a day of work until I was taken off the schedule two months later.)

I felt like I was still getting the runaround from them about what they did spiritually. I wanted them to give me details about what they did. How my soul pieces were returned, etc. These are the types of things that happen in a traditional soul retrieval. Marsha said that what they did was deeper than a soul retrieval. I had gone there for a traditional soul retrieval and I didn't get one. They couldn't answer my questions to a soul retrieval, because I hadn't gotten one. They weren't willing to share what they did or what had happened.

They were able to help answer the questions that had been going through my mind. I had asked about the panic attack that I had outside the cave. Kathryn said that I had been suffering from panic attacks all my life and I never knew it. I asked about having PTSD. Kathryn said that I did have PTSD. I had PTSD since I was a baby. When I asked about being drugged, they both agreed that my mother had given me cough syrup and alcohol as a child to keep me quiet. I have a memory of being with my mother and brothers in the hallway built-in cupboard. I remember asking why I wasn't getting cough syrup. I remember my mom saying that I didn't need any, because I wasn't sick anymore. I remember thinking way back then, that what my mother said didn't make sense. I was never sick when she gave me the cough syrup before.

I asked if there was any child pornography of me and they both said yes. They both said they picked up a lot of energy around this one. My Grandfather had taken pictures of me when he abused me. So yes, there was child pornography of me. I do have a memory of him having a camera in his office. I remember seeing the flash cube on the camera. If they existed, there would be no denying that they were of me. I have a significant strawberry birthmark on my buttocks, but she would still deny it. If I was able to produce pictures to my mother, she still wouldn't believe me. They both confirmed that my mother knew that my Grandfather had sexually abused me the day it happened. When she saw me, she decided not to deal with it. She had made a conscious choice to not deal with me or the situation. She couldn't admit it then and I doubt she would admit it now. In the end, I had gotten a better picture of how I was abused and neglected. Now I know that I had suffered from PTSD all my life. Having PTSD all your life you really don't know what normal is, because PTSD is your normal.

At the close of the meeting Marsha had made a lot of comments to me. She said that she was hoarse for five days after the soul retrieval. She was blaming me for her being hoarse. I didn't clearly understand what was expected of me on the soul retrieval. It wasn't clearly explained to me. She expressed that she felt I was ungrateful for her spooning me in the cave. She did offer, and I said yes, but now I get backlash over it? She said that I was one of the hardest people she had worked with, and made a reference to my behavior prior to starting the detox diet. I had all these reservations about it and wanted my questions answered before I started. I was shocked that she had said all these things. I was amazed at the lack of compassion that she had towards a client that went to her for healing. I was shocked that she would tell a client these things. I was shocked that she had a hard time answering my questions. I had asked questions to gain a better understanding of what was done in the soul retrieval. I wasn't being ungrateful or unappreciative as Marsha was seeing it. I was trying to understand what I had paid for and what exactly they did. Maybe Marsha didn't like the fact that I challenged her and asked questions. I don't know.

Marsha had brought up the intuitive seminar again and I told her that I would think about it. (They're intuitive, shouldn't they have known I wasn't going to go?) Marsha had suggested that I forget the story of the soul retrieval in the desert. I told her that I was writing a book about my experiences. Marsha brought up the money I owed and suggested that I give the remainder of what I owed to charity instead of them. She asked Kathryn's opinion and she didn't agree, nor did I. I wanted to be free and clear of them. I didn't want to owe them anything. I did not want to have any bad karma coming my way.

Marsha and Kathryn had sent me to a website where they held online meetings. They had wanted me to do an online weekly meeting with them and others. I felt that Marsha had been trying to build up the idea of her and Kathryn being my masters. I felt that she built up the idea of me going to work in their shop. I felt that she had 'hyped' up her shop by telling me that she had worked with many "A-listers" from Hollywood. For a little while, I did consider the idea of going to live in Taos. When the idea was waning for me, I decided that my area needed a healer more than Taos. I didn't have to go there to be a healer. I think I had decided on my trip back from Taos that I didn't need a master and that I was going to be my own master.

I think Marsha was a little disappointed, when I told her in that last meeting that I had found a local place to go. I was still getting this 'carrot on a stick' impression from them. In hindsight, I think that is part of the reason that they didn't answer all of my questions. Leave me hanging, so that I would come back for more. I was getting the impression that they were part of a cult and that these two were "recruiters." I never said that these two aren't spiritually gifted. They are both very gifted healers. I felt they had an underlying agenda to recruit.

15
Free Will

The new place I had found was called "Nourishment 4 the Soul" and it felt like I had come home. It was warm and welcoming. Not fake. Not pushy in any way, shape, or form. They were not for profit, which made me feel even better about going there. Although, I had decided that I was going to be my own master, I knew I could benefit from being around like-minded people. I knew I didn't need to go to the intuitive school to get a piece of paper to tell me that I was an intuitive. I went around for at least a month saying that "I didn't need a piece of paper to tell me I was a spiritual healer." I made a list of all the things that I thought would help me in becoming a spiritual healer. I was going to teach myself whatever I wanted to or needed to know. I was going to be very selective in who I chose to teach me. I had already taught myself a lot in a few short months while doing research online. There was no reason that I couldn't be my own master. I believe many Ascended Masters did not have Masters and they were self-taught.

I had a clear idea of the standards that I wanted to implement into my healing practice. I experienced too many healing practices that I didn't agree with. Those things I absolutely did not want to do. There aren't any standards of practice for healers. I had researched healing standards of practice, there are some that have complied standards. I feel

Master in the Making

that's great. The thing is that it will always boil down to the individual healer and their practice. I felt that if I had a master, they would influence my healing practices. I was still contemplative about what God was asking me to do in becoming a spiritual healer. The truth is that everybody on this planet can be a spiritual healer. Everybody on this planet is able to heal their own mind, body and soul. Not everybody has a desire to take this path or the desire to want to heal themselves. I knew I was going to move forward with becoming a healer, but it was going to be in my own time, and in my own way. I knew that I couldn't go through another spiritual abuse experience. I knew that there was a possibility that if I followed a master that I would be disappointed. I suspected that I wouldn't get what I wanted out of having a master. I had enough unanswered questions from working with healers. Those healers wouldn't tell me about what they had done. I knew that I had the answers. The answers were deep within me. I was the only one who had the answers to those questions. Nobody else could answer those questions for me.

    Since coming back from Taos, I have worked with a few healers locally where I sought out more healing. I haven't felt spiritually abused by any of them. One of the local healers agreed that something funky had been done when I had my first Reiki session. They saw intuitive evidence of that. Earlier this year I became a Reiki Master. I do believe now that Trisha put some intentions into the Reiki that were not necessarily for my best and highest good. Those intentions were forced upon me and they met with resistance. I believe that's why my body reacted in such a way and I had such a hard time detoxing. I must add this little story about becoming a Reiki Master. It's kind of funny that my Master Reiki Teacher couldn't print out my certificate and said, *"You don't need a piece of paper to tell you that you're a master."*

Like I had mentioned before, Parker still texts me from time to time. Earlier this year I had sensed that there was something more to Parker and I being soulmates. I sensed that we had practiced magic together in one of our shared lifetimes. I was sensing that there was something else I had to clear away. I still was feeling heartache for him and I wanted to feel relief. I had been working on breaking any ties that Parker and I had made in our past lives together. In the same week, I had gone for a unique healing experience with Chaz Pro. Chaz was visiting Nourishment 4 the Soul to do healings. The healing consisted of sound vibration. It was Reiki on steroids. I opted to do the hour-long session. During my session with Chaz, I had visions of things in the future; one that involved a death. I really don't like the ones revolving around death. I had a happy vision of being at a very festive celebration. I was dancing on the beach barefoot with my family. I had never felt so happy in my life as I did in that vision. I had only recently been able to see glimpses of things while I was on the healing table. I had a healing session with Pam prior to having a healing with Chaz. In the healing session with Pam, I had sat straight up and said that my dad was going to die soon. I had seen my father's face in my mind. That vision was a little off. Two weeks later my ex-father-in-law passed away.

While I was in my healing session with Chaz, I had the oddest sensation I had ever felt. It felt like my soul was rocking back and forth out of my body. It was a little

Master in the Making

unsettling. Before Chaz began the session, he asked what to focus on and I told him my physical vision had become bad. I was only focused on my vision in that healing. I had never met Chaz before and hadn't told anybody what I had been working on. I had been working on my past lives. When the session was over, Chaz asked me if I had felt my soul moving in and out of my body. He asked if I had recently been working on any past life issues. I told him I had been working on past life issues. He said that my soul was moving in and out of my body because of the past life work I was doing. It was a trippy healing experience. I feel that the session helped me. If I get the opportunity to do that again, I probably will.

As I was working on my past lives with Parker, I had the impression that we possibly had made a soul contract in one of our lifetimes that prevented us from moving on. One healer had said that we had a relationship like Romeo and Juliet in a past life. I assumed that is when we had made a soul contract with each other. Parker had texted me in May of this year and wanted to get together. I went and picked him up from his house. We were going to play the drums at my house. Parker hadn't had a drum set in years. When we were dating, we would go into Guitar Center and he would play. That day he came to my house and he was impressed by my playing. I had recently started taking lessons in December. We drank and went out to dinner. When we got back from dinner, I told him about my past life work and the soul contract. I asked him if he would help me out by ripping up the contract. He agreed. I asked him to imagine that he was ripping up the contract and then lighting it on fire with white fire light. I had already worked on ripping up the contract a couple of weeks prior. I had started to feel a lot better and relieved of my heartache for him. I felt he needed to do this in my presence. That visit with Parker was when I was truly done with Parker. Over the next week or two Parker called me, and he wanted to get back together with me. I had told him repeatedly that wouldn't happen. I had been telling him that for nearly a year and a half. In the last few phone conversations with him I got mean and really called him out on his bullshit. I was being more honest with myself and with him. I told him that I knew who he was and what he was about. I told him I knew he has a bunch of girls he sees. He asked how I knew that. By him asking how I knew, was just confirmation of my intuition. I had been telling him that my intuition had told me this all along. He didn't believe that and thought I had been spying on him. Honestly, I don't need to waste my time spying on him. I knew when I had made the decision to flirt in the beginning that he was a cad. I thought I would never hear from again, but nope he called me the next day.

As I was writing it dawned on me that I had waited nearly twenty-one years for my husband to change. With Parker I had waited four lifetimes for him to change. It was time that we were no longer bound to each other romantically from here on out. I had to "let go" and he has to "let go." I need to move on and find somebody who I don't have to change. I need to find somebody who loves me, appreciates me and wants to be with me. I deserve to be happy, appreciated and cared for. I think I'm long overdue in having this in my life. "Letting go" is one of my major lessons to learn in this lifetime. It's not coincidental that My Great Grandfather Larry, and the Grandfather who abused me, were used to illustrate to me how important it is to "let go." They were both in limbo and could not move. I still have some things to work on. I may have to "let go" of ever getting those repressed memories I so desperately wanted, and I will have to be okay with it. I'm not perfect. I'm a work in progress.

I want to say that I see where I have suffered in some ways from the generational karma. The "delusional darkness" and "everything is just fine" to being "stubborn" and "doing the task to the end, no matter what it takes." The generational karma, I can say are mental illnesses. I must admit that I have been suffering from it all my life. On the other side of that, I am slowly healing. You can't just flick a switch to make it go away. I have lived like this for almost forty-nine years and it takes time to heal all the wounds. It takes time to heal past life wounds. I know I have some work to do. Some who are more advanced on their path than my own may see where I need work. There are things that I still need to explore. I still have more healing to do within me.

My path has been rough. I'm sure other people have had it rougher. I'm sure there are thousands upon thousands of even more heart wrenching stories than my own. I know that there are more sad and tragic stories than mine. I know that there is a lot of pain out there in the world. My path to recovery and healing has been very unorthodox to some. Others may choose to take other paths to heal and that's okay, it's their path. From my experiences that I have gone through they have given me a foundation in how treat other people when I am a spiritual healer. There's still so much more to learn and I will never stop learning how to help and heal. I have a motto that I have not only lived by growing up, but one that came up while I was a Realtor. It is the "'Golden Rule:' Do unto others as you would have them do unto you." One thing that I know to be true is that when I am healing another person, I will not cause them added hurt in the process. I want my clients to completely understand what is going on and for me to have compassion toward them. I want them to know that I will be there if they need me. There are Reiki practitioners and master's out there who use their Reiki with other healing modalities. For example, some Reiki practitioners and master's do not disclose they are using Reiki while doing a massage session. So, the person who had gone in for a massage doesn't realize that they got a little something extra. I want my clients to know that I am using Reiki and what the intention for their healing session will always be for their highest and best interest.

    A couple of months ago I was getting the impression that I needed to look more into the shop in Taos. I felt I was done with Taos. I didn't understand why I was feeling pushed to do some research about the shop. I had gone to the website that Marsha and Kathryn had sent to me for the online meetings. It was owned by a corporation and that corporation was owned by their master. Then I researched to see who owned that shop in Taos. It was the very same corporation that their master owned. The research lead me to believe that they didn't own the shop like Marsha had said. I know I could be wrong about that even with my research. It is possible that the two of them may just have some interest in that corporation. Now it makes sense to me, why Marsha had roommates. My research didn't stop with finding out who owned the shop. I went a little further and googled their master's name with the word "cult." There were articles on

MASTER IN THE MAKING

the internet about lawsuits against their master and associates. It was what I had suspected all along. They were part of a cult. Some people may feel the need to have a master. That's their path. You can choose to follow a master, or you can be your own master. I choose to be my own master. I'm free and I am not a slave to a master. If people want to read or hear what I have to say about spiritual healing I'm okay with it. If they want me to be their master; I will teach, I will help, and I will heal. I will teach them that they are their own master, because the answers you seek in enlightenment are always hidden within the seeker.

You are your own Master!

Suggested Reading

http://wisdomwithin.co/files/The-8-Clair-Senses-a-visual-guide-to-the-spiritual-psychic-senses.pdf
lonerwolf.com
spiritualawakeningprocess.com

Essential Reiki - Diane Stein
Archangels & Ascended Masters - Doreen Virtue
The Four Agreements - Don Miguel Ruiz
Hands of Light - Barbara Ann Brennan
Repressed Memories: A Journey to Recovery from Sexual Abuse – Renee Fredrickson
If You Give a Pig a Pancake – Laura Numeroff

Master in the Making

About the Author

It was once said that Julie is *"Possibly the Most Interesting Woman in the World."* A single, tattooed mother who currently has temporary full custody of her two grown sons. 'The Julie's' native habitat is the Central Valley of California. She takes shelter in a small 1920's Craftsman bungalow with her Schnauzer, Duke. Sometimes the Julie may be spotted outside of her native habitat in one the Julie's favorite places, South Lake Tahoe.

Julie offers *"Woo Woo for Your Boohoo"* in her private practice as a Reiki Master and Spiritual Healer. She quit her day job and is recovering from her time working in Real Estate. Prior to being a Realtor, Julie was a self-employed virtual office assistant telecommuting to exotic places, such as Ohio, Pennsylvania and Texas. She also did a short stint as a contracted graphic designer and self-employed web designer. Julie studied at Modesto Junior College and received an A.A. in General Studies and an A.S. in Computer Graphics Applications. Everything else Julie has learned has been by experience or from the internet.

Julie's most recent writing can be found in the Anthologies, *"Warrior Women with Angel Wings Illuminating Your Joy,"* and *"Reading Between the Signs."*

Aside from writing, Julie takes weekly drum lessons and last performed with the rock and roll band Funk Haus. Funk Haus disbanded after only two gigs.

Master in the Making

Find Julie inside the electronics you are using:
Facebook: julie.a.guthrie.smulson
Twitter & Instagram: jagsmulson
Word Press: http://masterinthemakingblog.wordpress.com
Websites:
www.masterinthemaking.com
www.spiritualalchemyenergytransfigurations.com

www.ingramcontent.com/pod-product-compliance
Lightning Source LLC
Chambersburg PA
CBHW052031070526
44584CB00016B/1988